A History of Wootton
Bedfordshire

HISTORY OF WOOTTON
BEDFORDSHIRE

First published 2002 by
C&C Printers
4-6 Houghton Road
Bedford
Bedfordshire
MK42 9HQ

Printed by

BEDFORDSHIRE
THE HISTORIC PARISHES (c1880)

Legend:

────	Modern County Boundary
────	Historic Parish Boundary
Linslade (Bucks)	Whole or parts of Parishes transferred to Bedfordshire since c1880
●●●●●	Peculiar Jurisdictions

Parish and place labels (as shown on map):

Shelton, Tilbrook, Dean, Yielden, Melchbourne, Swineshead (Hunts), Pertenhall, Little Staughton, Wymington, Farndish, Podington, Knotting, Riseley, Keysoe, Souldrop, Sharnbrook, Odell, Bletsoe, Bolnhurst, Colmworth, Eaton Socon, Harrold, Felmersham, Chellington, Milton Ernest, Thurleigh, Little Barford, Carlton, Pavenham, Oakley, Ravensden, Wilden, Roxton, Turvey, Stevington, Clapham, Goldington, Renhold, Great Barford, Blunham, Tempsford, Everton, Tetworth (Hunts), Bromham, BEDFORD, Bidden-ham, Willington, Mogerhanger, SANDY, Potton, Stagsden, Kempston, Cople, Cardington, Northill, Sutton, Cockayne Hatley, Wrestling-worth, Elstow, Eastcotts, Old Warden, Eyeworth, Wootton, Cranfield, Marston Moretaine, Houghton Conquest, Wilshamstead, Haynes, Southill, BIGGLESWADE, Dunton, Salford, Lidlington, Hulcote, Ridgmont, Husborne Crawley, Kitchend, AMPTHILL, Chicksands Priory, Clophill, Compton, Clifton, Longford, Edworth, Aspley Guise, Stepping-ley, Maulden, Silsoe, Meppershall, Henlow, Astwick, Stotfold, Wavendon (Bucks), Woburn, Eversholt, Flitwick, Flitton, Pulloxhill, Grovebury, Upper Stondon, Astley, Potsgrove, Milton Bryan, Tingrith, Westoning, Harlington, Higham Gobion, Shillington, Heath & Reach, Battlesden, TODDINGTON, Streatley, Harlington, Linslade (Bucks), LEIGHTON BUZZARD, Eggington, Hockliffe, Tilsworth, Chalgrave, Sundon, Stanbridge, Billington, Houghton Regis, LUTON, Totternhoe, Eaton Bray, Dunstable, Kensworth (Herts), Coddington (Beds), Coddington (Herts), Whipsnade, Studham (Beds), Studham (Herts)

Numbered references:

1. Colworth
2. Shefford Hardwick
3. Shefford
4. Holwell
5. Higham Gobion
6. Harlington
7. Westoning
8. Houghton Regis
9. Studham

Bedfordshire and Luton Archives Service (Culture and Environment Group, Bedfordshire County Council)

Contents

Illustrations

Introduction

In the year 2000, Wootton held a Millennium Week with a large variety of events organised to cater for most tastes and interests. One of the most successful was the exhibition of old photographs of the village, on show all week at the Baptist Church. From there, the photographs spent some time on display in Wootton library and as a result, the idea of writing a history of Wootton, using some of these photos, was born. An appeal in the Wootton News brought together a group of interested people and so the project began. Some two years later with a lot of hard work, the final history book has been published. The contributors are villagers with an interest in history rather than professional historians, and have spent time reading old records, talking to older residents and gathering information where they can. Wherever possible, original sources have been used, to verify the facts in the book but should there be any mistakes or errors, we apologise now!!

The contributors are:- Arthur Brittain, Mary Dearing, Rena Jenkins, Susan Lambert, Cliff Minney, Vivienne Minney, Dina Smith, Mark Smith, Mike Smith, Dorothy Warman and Gordon Willey.

Our thanks to the following people who gave us help and shared their memories:- Sid Cook, Cecil Caves, William Cook, Rick and Jean Sherwood, Molly Foster, Doris Hutchings, Constance Robinson, Denis Billing, Peggy Boston, Hugh Copperwheat, Brenda Copperwheat, Bruce Arnold, John Gates, Frank Cook, Cicely McKeegan, Alec Head,

Jane Bowling, Paul Lowe, Neville Medcalf, Jean Lewin, Tessa Harfield, Hilary Hull and Yasmine Cargill.

A big thankyou to everyone who kindly gave their permission to reproduce their photographs.

Thanks also to Bedfordshire County Council and the Millennium Fund for grants towards this publication and to the Wootton Millennium Committee for allowing the proceeds of the Millennium Week to be used to help publish this book.

Credit for this publication is also due, in no small measure, to our printers and publishers, C&C Printers of Houghton Road, Bedford, and in particular, to Chris Marotta and Gary Markham. Without their advice, hard work and attention to detail, this book would not be such a professional presentation. A sincere thankyou.

The quilt on the cover of this book was made to enter the "Our Village" quilting competition organised by Bedfordshire Rural Communities Charity in 1994 and is now on display in Wootton library. Those taking part were:- Ann Allen, Sandy Anderson, Sarah Billington, Irene Clifton, Eleanor Farmer, Margaret Greenhalgh, Basil Gurney, Trixie Gurney, Muriel Haddon, Gill Head, Jane Helliwell, Mick Henderson, Hilary Hull, Gwen Lambert, Debbie McGolpin, Barbara Morall, Sam MacQueen, Dorothy Rickets, Nadine Sneath, Victoria Sneath, Sally Snelson, Janet Southworth, Lesley Waller, Dorothy Warman, Archie Watkins, pupils from Wootton Lower School and Wootton Guides and Brownies.

In The Beginning

A Very Old Place

Wootton has been a village for well over 1000 years. It was a large and well-established place when the first Norman King, William the Conqueror became King of England. The first historical record of the village of Wootton is in the Domesday Book in 1086. Wootton was probably a village or a group of farmsteads for several hundred years before that. Some Roman pottery has been found at Keeley Corner and in the churchyard.

Aelmer, Lord of the Manor

The first recorded Lord of the Manor of Wootton was Aelmer during the reign of Edward the Confessor, 1042 to 1066. Aelmer owed allegiance to Tolsti, Earl of Northumbria. Tolsti's brother, Harold, became King of England on the death of Edward the Confessor in 1066. Tolsti himself, died at the Battle of Stamford Bridge, shortly before Harold was defeated by William the Conqueror at the Battle of Hastings. By the time of the Domesday Book, William had made Albert of Lorraine, Lord of the Manor of Wootton.

Domesday Book

The Domesday Book, in translation, says of Wootton:-

In Redbornstoke Hundred, Albert of Lorraine holds Wootton himself.
It answers for 10 hides.
Land for 11 ploughs.
In lordship 2 hides, 3 ploughs there.
20 villagers have 7 ploughs; an eighth possible.
6 slaves.
Meadow for 5 ploughs.
Woodland, 400 pigs.
Value £10; Value when acquired £8. Before 1066 £10.15s.
Before 1066, Aelmer, Earl Tosti's man, held this manor. He could sell.

Farming Practice 1000 Years Ago

Every farmer in the village had to co-operate with the others. Not only did they share ploughs and teams of oxen, to work their own strips in the common fields, but they were also directed by the Steward when working on the fields worked by the Lord of the Manor and his Steward. The farmers would have to agree common dates to start ploughing, sowing and harvesting, and especially when to exclude or allow animals to graze the stubble on the common fields. One function of the Lord's Manor Court, which his tenants attended, was to decide these important matters, arbitrate on disputes and fine or punish defaulters. These fines were a lucrative source of income for the Lord of the Manor.

Size of the Village

By 1086, there were 20 farmers living in Wootton. These farmers rented land from the Lord of the Manor, who held the village from the King.

There was about 1300 acres of cornfield in the Parish, worked by 10 plough teams. About one third of the Parish was arable land for growing other crops and woods covered a further sixth of the Parish, used to support 400 pigs. Meadows covered a thirtieth of the Parish. In all, more than half the land was cornfields, permanent pasture and managed woodland. The rest, just under half, was wasteland, used for rough grazing, collecting firewood and wild fruit. The fields in the village were laid out as large common fields. Each farmer rented several strips in different parts of the fields.

At the time of the Domesday Book, in 1086, about 120 people lived in the village. In addition to the 20 farmers or villagers and their families, there were 6 servants or slaves and, maybe the Lord of the Manor, but more likely, his Steward.

Albert of Lorraine rented out about four-fifths of the farmland to these 20 tenant farmers. He farmed himself 360 acres, described as land for 3 ploughs, which was almost one-third of the fields in the Parish. The labour used on Albert's own land was not hired but was the labour services of the tenant farmers of the village. Instead of paying money rent, the tenant farmers had to provide several days of ploughing of the Lord's land, using their own oxen, as well as road mending, carriage, and harvesting. These services were onerous and could take up to three days every week of the year.

These farmers were secure tenants and although they could not sell their lands, their farms could be inherited by their heirs and therefore there was a strong incentive to improve the land by draining, manuring it, removing stones and not to overgraze.

Animals, Ploughs and Crops

There were over 80 oxen in Wootton in 1086, organised into 10 plough teams. The Lord of the Manor owned three teams and the farmers would probably own part of a plough team and cultivate about 60 or so acres. In addition to oxen, each farmer would have one or more cows for milk, several pigs, chickens, geese, possibly a horse and some sheep. The cultivated land was divided into two large fields or groups of fields. Corn was grown in each field on alternate years, the field lying fallow in the intervening year. This cycle of cultivation was based on spring ploughing and sowing. After the Harvest, the animals continued to graze all winter and through the fallow of the following year, manuring the land and allowing it to recover. This system of farming continued until the lands were enclosed in the seventeen and early eighteen hundreds.

The weather was warmer at the time of the Domesday Book than it is now, some one to two degrees centigrade higher. The period 950 to 1300 AD was known as the "Little Optimum" and Wootton would have had the climate of a village in the Loire valley. The growing season was two or three weeks longer than now.

About a third of the cultivated land in Wootton was meadow. After the hay crop in the early summer, the animals would also be allowed to graze this meadowland. At all times of the year, animals grazed the verges and other wasteland, which was used as permanent pasture. Pigs grazed in the woods all the year round. Fruit and vegetables would be grown in the villagers' gardens.

Bread

Wheat, rye and barley grown in the fields provided flour for bread which was the staple food in villages such as Wootton. There was no Mill in the village at this time so corn must have been taken to a neighbouring village to be ground.

Most villagers, except the very poor, would have kept a cow, or goats or sheep for milk. Cheese could be stored all winter and bread and cheese was the standard fare when working all day in the fields.

A Villager's Diet

Houses in the village had large garden plots, which were used to grow vegetables as well as housing the farm animals. Vegetables grown included onions, leeks, celery, radish, shallots, parsnips, carrots, garlic, cabbage, lettuce, and the herbs, parsley, dill, chervil, marigold, coriander and poppy. Fruit trees also provided apples, plums and cherries. Figs, quince, peach and mulberry were also grown in southern England, as well as pears, damsons, grapes, strawberries, and various nuts such as walnut, chestnut, almonds and hazelnuts.

Honey from bees was the main source of sweetness and the bee's wax could be used to make good quality candles. These were much better, but far more expensive, than the tallow tapers made from animal fat.

One of the staple dishes was pottage, a broth or stock eaten every day. It comprised mostly vegetables with some meat, boiled in water with herbs for flavouring and cereals and pulses to add body. There were many different recipes for pottage, including leek, pease pottage or a vegetable version made with cabbage, lettuce, onion and garlic.

Fish was also part of the diet. Fresh fish caught in the rivers such as salmon, trout, grayling, bream or tench, was available. Monasteries would have fishponds and so to would large estates. Fish could also be brought by barge up the Great Ouse from the coast. Herring was salted or pickled on the North Sea coast to preserve them for travel inland and to keep during the winter. Dried cod was an alternative sea fish.

The Manors of Wootton

Albert of Lorraine was not Lord of the Manor of Wootton for very long. The manor soon passed into the hands of the Sheriff of Bedford, de Beauchamp, Baron of Bedford and a member of one of the three most powerful families in the county. The 2000 acres of fields, meadows and woodlands in the Manor of Wootton was only part of his property in several parishes in Bedfordshire. The de Beauchamps owned Wootton until 1245.

In 1245, the last surviving male heir, John de Beauchamp, died at the Battle of Evesham. The Manor of Wootton and his property rights within the village were divided between his widow, his sisters, his nieces, and other relatives. Within 50 years, what had once been one large Manor had been transformed into nine separate Manors. There were some other small landowners with property in the village, in addition to tenant farmers. Some of the Manors were relatively small. The Manor of Pilling in Wootton, which was owned by the Knights Hospitaller by 1247, was 146 acres of fields, pastures and woods. Studleys Manor comprised one house, two cottages and 58 acres of land. Each Manor had its own Lord, so there were several people with the title "Lord of the Manor", but they were only Lord of their own land and manor. They were not the Lord of the Village of Wootton.

Major Landowners in Wootton

By the end of the 13th century, the major landowners were:

Bosums Manor –	Roger Lestrange, husband of Maud, sister of John de Beauchamp.
Wootton Manor –	John de Botetcourt, heir to Beatrice, sister of John de Beauchamp.
	Elizabeth Hoobury, niece of John de Beauchamp.
Wootton Hoo –	Simon de Patishull, husband of Mabel, niece of John de Beauchamp Michael Picot, then Ralph Payne, husband of Joan, niece of John de Beauchamp.
Pilling Rousberry –	William le Rous.
Pilling in Wootton –	Knights Hospitaller, later called Pilling Shingay.
Studleys –	St. Edwards family, as dowry of Alice, the wife of John St. Edwards. The land went to the Studley Family on Alice's marriage to Thomas Studley about 1318.
Canons –	Became known as this after the Dissolution

16

of the Monasteries, belonged to Newnham Priory.

Culy (Keeley) – Does not appear in any records until 1474. Owned then by the Neville family.

Wootton Shelton – Belonged to the Priory of Caldwell, now in the Parish of Marston Moreteyne.

Medieval Wootton

Growth

The population of Wootton grew steadily until the beginning of the 14th century. By 1300, there were four times as many people in the village compared to when the Domesday survey took place. By the 1309 Tax Rolls List, there were 89 taxpayers in Wootton. The population would have been at least 500 people, living in more than 100 households. This Tax was levied by King Edward II and Parliament on all land worth 20 shillings or more a year. Also taxed were indications of wealth such as personal possessions and armour. The resulting lists produced gives the names of the richest households and the amount of tax paid. There would also be a number of poorer households, not listed who paid no tax.

The two largest taxpayers in Wootton in 1309 were Willmo Le Rous of Pilling Rousberry (now part of Stewartby) and Johanne Bottourte, of Wootton Manor. The 22 families, who paid more than three shillings and six pence in tax, are listed in Appendix 1.

As the population grew, a shortage of cultivated land developed. Younger sons would have had to find new land to farm, or new employment. Much rough grazing was brought into cultivation. A number of smallholdings, often known as "closes" were carved out of common fields or wasteland.

Land and Leases

There was a complex market in land in 1300. Lands held by tenants of the manor, copyhold or freehold, were often let at an economic rent to someone else; a sub-tenant, whose existence was not in the cognisance of the manorial system. Although the manor survived, it was in a variety of ways, being by-passed.

Manorial customs varied enormously. Broadly speaking, freeholders could do what they liked with their land, although they still had to pay some dues and fines to their lord of the manor. Copyholders were mainly customary tenants who held their land by inheritance or for specified periods of years. Copyholders paid fines to the manorial lord to take over the tenancy. Tenants at will, who held land entirely at the will of the lord, were usually poor cottagers, or were squatters on the wastelands. Their leases and rights depended not upon manorial law or custom, but upon the Common Law.

In many cases, the economic lease was already the crucial element in the landlord's income. By the end of the 15th century, serfdom, villeinage and labour services were largely defunct in England, although some examples of the survival of villeinage can be found throughout the 16th century.

Obligations to the Crown

In addition to rent and service to the Lord of the Manor, the people of Wootton had many other obligations to the Crown. One of these was service in the army. The feudal military obligation, that barons and knights were summoned to give military service to the King in return for land, was gradually replaced by armies composed of the King's household, volunteers, paid soldiers and mercenaries. But the obligation to serve in the County Militia for home defence, remained an important duty of all men.

Successive Kings and Parliaments arranged for the defence of

England by raising permanent armies and by organising a county militia from all able bodied men in each county. The County Militia provided the majority of troops available to Henry VIII and Queen Elizabeth I in their wars with Spain. If the Spanish Armada had landed an army in 1588, the militiamen of Wootton would have been mobilised as part of the Bedfordshire militia, to meet the invasion. The militia also served as police or bailiffs when required by the Sheriff or the Justices.

All able-bodied men between the ages of 16 and 60 were required to serve in the county militia. Nobles and their households, clergy and the disabled, were exempt. The militia was mustered at least once a year for inspection of equipment and training. A muster list of 1539 gives the names of all the men of Wootton in the militia. See Appendix 2.

The Muster Rolls for the Bedfordshire County Militia for 1539 listed 35 men in Wootton, which implies a population of about 200 people in 40 households.

New Farming Methods

Although there was no active market in the buying and selling of leases, many families chose to improve there farming methods, to support their extended families. The amount of food grown was helped by the change to the three-field rotation of crops. Corn was grown for two successive years and in the third year, the land lay fallow. A mill was built in the Manor of Pilling in Wootton, later known as Pilling Shingay. This would have been a windmill as there was no suitable stream available.

The use of horses for ploughing grew in late medieval times. Often mixed teams of horses and oxen were used, the horses led the teams, adding speed to the oxen's strength. Although fed on the more expensive grain, horses were more flexible. Climate changes after 1300 produced cooler weather. Wootton, like the rest of England, suffered a series of cold, wet winters and poor harvests, particularly in the years from 1314 to 1317.

By 1339, there were only 47 taxpayers. The total tax paid in the

1339 Lay Subsidy was less than the amount levied 30 years earlier. Tax receipts were down throughout the country, due to a mixture of poor harvests and tax evasion. It is therefore likely the population of Wootton decreased.

The fortunes of many families changed in those 30 years. The Bottuorte family had left Wootton Manor, and the le Rous family of Pilling Rousberry was reduced from the largest taxpayer, down to the thirty-eighth. The Astel family had become the largest taxpayers.

In England as a whole, the people, weakened by food shortages, were vulnerable to illness and epidemics. The plague of the Black Death reached London in 1348 and Wootton, by 1349. The next major epidemic was not until the Plague in 1604, when 48 people died including six people from the Cocks family and five from the Stanbridge family.

New Foods, Changing Tastes – Late Medieval

The Crusaders, returning from the Middle East, introduced spinach into England in the 12th century, and from 1290, oranges and lemons began to be imported. Cows' milk began to replace that of sheep and goats in the 10th century. Sugar arrived in Europe as early as the 10th century, probably from Persia or Egypt but it was insignificant until the later Middle Ages. It was only with the development of plantations in the West Indies in the 17th century, that sugar began to replace honey in the English diet.

Early Enclosures and Wool

The price of wool was high from 1450 to 1520. During this period, many farmers increased the number of sheep in their flocks. In Bedfordshire and other midland counties, some manors and landowners enclosed their open cornfields and communal grazing, to provide more permanent pasture for sheep.

The Old Tithe Barn, unfortunately demolished in 1955 by the Bedford R.D.C. Probably dating back architecturally to the early 1500's, it would have been used to store the tithes given to the Vicar, of grain and other produce.

The Old Lock Up used to stand just outside the churchyard on land belonging to Wootton House. It was demolished in the 1970's and the door was rescued by Bob Lunniss and can still be seen at his former cottage half way up Cause End Road.

Although wool was an important product, and manure was vital for the cornfields, Wootton remained a village of mainly mixed farms. Wool was never dominant to the extent it was in Yorkshire, Suffolk and the Cotswolds.

Farmland

In Wootton the common wasteland, previously only used for rough grazing or firewood, continued to be brought into cultivation. A number of smallholdings, often known as "closes", were carved out of common fields or wasteland. In 1490, Thomas Mitchell, of Pulloxhill, sold Yppinges Close, in Wootton. Another close was known as "John Smythes". In 1596, in the Manor of Pilling Rousberry, Thomas Terle sold enclosures called "Bowes", "Gamers" and the "Great Hayes".

Food in Tudor England

Apples, plums, pears, cherries and strawberries had grown in England since Roman times. In the 16th century, gardeners began growing quinces, apricots, raspberries and melons. Dried fruits such as raisins, currants, prunes, figs and dates were imported luxuries.

New World Food

Tomatoes were introduced into England from Mexico in Elizabethan times and kidney beans arrived from Peru. The potato arrived from Chile and the Andes and by the end of the 17th century, had become a major part of the working class diet, especially in areas where oats rather than wheat, was grown. The turkey, a native of Mexico and Central America, was brought across in the 1540's and sugar began to replace honey when the plantations were established in the West Indies, in the 17th century. By the mid 17th century, tea was being imported from China.

Population Pressure and Poverty

In Tudor England, the growth in population aggravated problems of unemployment and poverty. In Parliament, in 1573, there were complaints of the great increase in "rogues, vagabonds and thieves" and of a "multitude of beggars." In 1552 Poor Relief became the responsibility of the parish and in 1601, the Poor Law Act introduced a Property tax, to be used to support poor people in their own houses. In 1834, the Poor Law Act introduced centralised Workhouses and outdoor relief was abolished.

The River Ouse: A Route to the World

From the Saxon times, the River Ouse was an important route for merchants and soldiers. There was a Saxon settlement in Kempston, in a strategic position across lines of communication.

The river network gave Wootton farmers and Bedford merchants the opportunity to sell cash crops, wool, agricultural by-products and the surplus from good harvests in a wider market. From Saxon times, the River Ouse was navigable as far as Huntingdon and St. Ives, and passable by small boats as far as Willington and Bedford. In the 13th century, King's Lynn was the third most important port in England. Ships travelled regularly to Holland, Germany, Scandinavia and the Baltic ports.

Stone and timber for the cathedral at Ely and the Cambridge colleges was carried by barge from quarries in Northamptonshire along the tributaries of the Ouse and the network of drainage canals in the Ouse, Nene and Cam valleys. The stone used to build Wootton Church would have travelled by both wagon and by barge from the quarry.

By the end of the 16th century, coal was important for fires in the blacksmiths ships and as domestic fuel in the houses of the merchants and the gentry. Coal was brought by ship from Newcastle and North East England to King's Lynn, where it was off-loaded into barges for transport to Peterborough, Northamptonshire, Bedfordshire, Cambridgeshire and Norfolk. By 1640, the River Ouse was navigable by barge as far as Great Barford.

Evidence that Bedford was regarded as the "Port" for this area, is shown by the name of the old road out of Wootton called "Potters or Potty Cross", the road to the "port".

Wootton House
Its History and Ownership

The Beginnings of Wootton

A village, such as Wootton, whose name ends in the syllable "TON" usually indicates that the area has been settled since Saxon times. In fact, the layout of Wootton is typically Saxon. The whole area then would have been covered by woodland and the Saxons would clear small areas, settle, build shelters and begin to farm and graze their livestock. The various "ends" in Wootton, Hall End, Keeley etc. are evidence of this.

The Victoria County History of Bedfordshire, published in 1912, gives a very clear account of the ownership of the nine different Manors of Wootton, including Keeley, Bossums, Canons, Pillinge (the modern Stewartby), Studleys and Wootton, between the taking of the Domesday Survey in 1086 when Albert of Lorraine, a henchman of William the Conqueror was the landowner, and the early 16th century. The Manors all formed part of various different wealthy family estates and were inherited or formed parts of marriage settlements, for some 400 years. Each Manor would have consisted of a main farmhouse, adjacent farm buildings and cottages for the farm labourers. Two examples of the farmhouses still existing today are Keeley Grange and Bourne End House. The owners of the various Manors simply had the rents from their lands collected, usually by a Bailiff, and there is no evidence to suggest any of them actually lived in the village.

However, in the reign of Henry VIII in 1514, the Manor of Bossums, some 500 acres, made up of 100 acres of meadows, 300 of pasture and 100 acres of furze and heath with its main farmhouse at Bourne End, was purchased by a wealthy City of London merchant draper, Sir George Monoux. There were six tofts (farm houses) and 20 messuages (cottages) on the land. He had been Sheriff of London in 1509 and became Lord Mayor of London in 1515. His home was Walthamstow, where even today there is a college named after him. He was obviously a wealthy man and at one time, owned land in 10 different English counties. He endowed a Grammar School in Walthamstow in 1527 and also gave money for the establishment of Almshouses there. He died in 1543, and he and his wife, Dame Dorothy, are commemorated in the Parish Church of Walthamstow.

The estates passed eventually to Lewis Monoux, in 1593, the heir of Sir George's nephew, Richard. It is likely that Lewis was the first Monoux to live in Wootton, his widowed mother was buried here in 1609 and his sister was married here in 1618. Lewis died in 1628, was succeeded by his son, Humphrey, who increased the estate by purchasing more land in the Manor of Wootton between 1639 and 1666, from Lord Carlisle. These new purchases included the land where the present Wootton House stands.

These were troubled times, the Civil War was imminent. There were already difficulties developing between Parliament and the King, Charles I. The first 11 years of his reign were relatively quiet until in 1635, he began to levy ship money on inland counties. Humphrey Monoux, who was the Sheriff of Bedfordshire, managed with his successor, to collect almost all of the £3000 required. In the following years the Sheriffs were not nearly so successful. By 1640, when the head on clash between the Parliamentarians and the Royalists came, Bedfordshire had nine MP's, in Parliament, seven of whom were active Parliamentarians. The close by Roman Catholic landowner, Sir Lewis Dyve of Bromham, was an active Royalist. There was a garrison at Newport Pagnell and skirmishes took place at Ampthill, Dunstable and even on Bedford Bridge, between soldiers of the two opposing armies. Most landowners wished for a quiet life and Humphrey Monoux was fortunate in obtaining a warrant excluding him from having to quarter soldiers.

After the King was beheaded in 1649, many prominent landowners either withdrew or were secluded from Parliament. Humphrey Monoux, who had been a member of the Bedfordshire Committee, also took a back seat. At the Restoration of the Monarchy in 1660, when Charles II came to the throne, Humphrey Monoux was created a Baronet, possibly suggesting he had Royalist sympathies!

Sir Humphrey Monoux died in 1666 and was succeeded by his son, also Sir Humphrey. He had married an heiress, Ann Cotton of Conington in Huntingdonshire and was able, with the help of her large marriage settlement, to purchase even more land. 1669 saw lands in Cardington added to the estate and in 1670, a substantial estate was purchased in Sandy. As a local Magistrate, Sir Humphrey was signatory to John Bunyan's arrest in 1674. The building of Wootton House probably dates from soon after Humphrey's elevation to Baronet, as being a prominent and respected local landowner, he would want to have a suitable residence to reflect his status. In the 1674 Hearth Tax Returns, Wootton House was taxed on nine hearths, still a relatively modest house, but by far the largest property in the village.

The Monoux family continued to take an active role in County affairs, spending time at both of their estates in Wootton and Sandy, Sandy Place being built in 1752. The Parish Records for both Sandy and Wootton show a large number of their Baptisms, Marriages and Burials. They served on such august bodies as Turnpike Trusts, as Members of Parliament for Bedford, as Sheriff of the County and as Magistrates. The third Sir Humphrey, together with the Duke of Bedford, was a great supporter of the Races in Bedford, both sponsoring races, and entering his own racehorses. Races took place at a number of venues in the County, as late as 1854 in Dunstable and flat racing took place for over 150 years at Race Meadow, near Cow Bridge, between Elstow and Kempston. From 1730 to 1740, it was difficult to attract entries but in 1733, a purse of 50 guineas was put up and Sir Humphrey won with his gelding, "Foxhunter", and again in 1734. Meetings ceased in 1740 but were revived again in 1753 by the Duke of Bedford.

Sir Philip Monoux, son of the second Sir Humphrey, succeeded to the title in 1685, dying some 22 years later and he did not increase the estates. His son, the third Sir Humphrey, was only five at his father's death. He bought small parcels of land in Hall End and Sandy, was a strong Jacobite supporter and was not active politically in the County. He died with no children to inherit, and the Baronetcy passed to Sir Philip Monoux, his cousin, in 1757. Sir Philip was a Major in the Bedfordshire Militia and served as Sheriff in 1763. He married Elizabeth, daughter of Ambrose Riddell, of Eversholt and had one son and four daughters. In 1805 aged 69, he died and was succeeded by his son, another Sir Philip. He only survived his father by four years, dying unmarried in 1809. The title then went to yet another Sir Philip, a kinsman, who was a clerk in holy orders and also unmarried. He died in 1814 and the Baronetcy then expired, there being no more direct male heirs.

The Four Monoux Sisters Inherit

All the estates, houses, farms and small parcels of land then reverted to the four surviving daughters of the Sir Philip who had died in 1805. The eldest, Mary, inherited the largest amount including most of Wootton. Her sister, Lucy, inherited the remainder of Wootton plus lands at Kempston Hardwick, Cardington and Turvey; the estates in Sandy went to Frances and the fourth daughter, Judith, inherited the land in Nottinghamshire. By this time, Mary, formerly the widow of John Payne, was now married to J.F. Buckworth. From her first husband, the eldest son of Sir Gillies Paynes of Roxton, she inherited a sugar plantation in St. Kitts, an island in the West Indies. Eventually, on her death, the estate passed to her grandson, Sir Coventry Payne. The Enclosure Map of Wootton in 1838 clearly shows the large holdings of land of the two sisters, Mary and Lucy.

(left)

The wedding of Harold Edward Churton Ditmas and Sybil Harriet Monoux Payne on 5th December 1906, in London.

(below)

Wootton House, built of red brick, late in the 17th century.

31

The Payne Family

Life in Victorian England for owners of country estates was not too easy. There were several severe agricultural depressions and in Wootton, it was no exception. The estate was heavily mortgaged and to ease this, Wootton House itself was often leased out, to bring in extra revenue. The estates in the West Indies were also not financially successful. When Sir Coventry Payne died in 1879, his successor, Sir Philip Payne was only 15 and still being tutored by Rev. Augustus Orlebar of Willington. He continued his education, finally attending Magdalen College, Cambridge whilst his sister, Henrietta was tutored at home by a Governess, Miss Schroder.

Despite the poor economic climate, Sir Coventry Payne had added to the estate, by purchasing Berry Farm in 1870. However, in his will he obliged his son, Sir Philip, to provide an annual sum of £500 to his sister, Henrietta. This proved impossible. In 1874, the estate was valued at £1800 and by 1892; this had dropped to £1300. To ease the burden at home, the estates in St. Kitts were at first leased out and then finally sold for £7500 in 1892. In 1885, the lands in Eversholt, previously inherited by Lucy Monoux in 1814, reverted back to the Wootton estate and Sir Philip Payne.

The Doyne-Ditmas Family

Sir Philip Payne married Winifred Doyne, daughter of a wealthy Irish family from Dublin, in 1880. At this time, a large sum of money was settled on any children of the marriage by the Doyne family, but could not be used to help the finances of the estate. As the decline in agriculture continued, circumstances did not improve for Sir Philip. The lifestyle the family enjoyed, such as private rail carriages to the seaside in Norfolk, overseas holidays etc. could not be supported from the income from the estate. Eventually his daughter, Sybil, who had married Major Ditmas in 1906, bought the estate for £7776 5s. 8d. including the contents of the house. This enabled Sir Philip to purchase an annuity and he then continued to live at Bourne End. Wootton House was leased out until 1920 when Sybil became her father's tenant. Her husband, in 1918 had added the name Doyne, (Sybil's grandmother's name), to their surname and was then always known as Major Doyne-Ditmas.

The Break-up of the Estate

Unfortunately, Mrs Doyne-Ditmas could still not make the estate pay and finally, in 1927, most of the estate was put up for auction. Some parts remained in the family; Wood Farm was sold in 1944 to a daughter of Sybil, Mrs Eyvor Pelham Reid, Bourne End in 1948 and Berry Farm in 1949. Mrs Doyne-Ditmas and her husband purchased Kempston Manor in 1928 and then in 1935, moved to the Clock House in Kempston. On her husband's death, Sybil returned to Wootton and lived the remainder of her life in Cause End Cottage.

Later Occupants of Wootton House

Sir Philip was widowed in 1918 when Lady Winifred died, aged 57. He himself lived on until 1935 when he was 76. Wootton House has had numerous occupants since the 1870's, many with connections to the military. By 1888, Colonel, the Honourable Robert Villiers Dillon, RHA, MP lived there. By 1920, the Doyne-Ditmas family had moved in and were there until 1928 when Captain, the Right Honourable William George Arthur Ormesby Gore MP and his wife, Lady Beatrice became the new owners. In 1940, the owner was Lt. Colonel, the Honourable Thomas George Breadalbane Morgan-Grenville DSO, MC. Colonel Morgan-Grenville took the role of Lord of the Manor seriously, allowed fetes and garden parties in the grounds of the house and played a full and active part in village life, being amongst other things, patron of the local Branch of the British Legion.

The Recent Years

On the death of Colonel Morgan-Grenville in 1965, the house and lands went up for sale and were bought by local Clapham farmer, Mr Edward Stratford, for around £20,000. His daughter, Mrs Mollie Foster, recollects that he was concerned that he might have overstretched his budget with this purchase. He was pleased to be able to re-sell the house within the year, realising almost the total he had originally paid for the land as well. The new owner was the writer, Quentin Crewe, and his wife, the novelist Angela Huth. During this time, there was much entertaining, and Mrs Doris Hutchings, who worked for both Colonel Morgan-Grenville and Quentin Crewe, can remember that visitors included Princess Margaret and her husband, Anthony Armstrong-Jones, Dudley Moore, Bamber Gascoigne and the author, Jocelyn Stephens. Interestingly, the family of Mrs Hutchings' husband had come to live and work in Wootton from Essex in the mid 1800's when Sir Coventry Payne moved from that county, to inherit the estate. Anthony Armstrong Jones, later Lord Snowdon, was the designer of the wheel chair used by Quentin Crewe and it was during his residence, that a lift was installed in the house. The household had a number of staff, a cook, chauffeur, gardener, maids and a nanny for the Crewe's daughter, Candida. Latterly, the house has been the offices for four national building companies, Bousteads, Winton Hayes, Wheatley Homes and Beazer Homes, and finally, in the year 2000, it has once again become a family home.

Memories of my Grandmother, Mrs Sybil Doyne-Ditmas by Mrs Tessa Harfield

Mrs Harfield wrote the following couple of paragraphs about her Grandmother:-

"My Grandmother, Sybil Doyne-Ditmas, was the last Lady of the Manor of Wootton until the estate was sold in 1927. When my grandfather died she moved into Cause End Cottage, where myself and my sisters often used to visit her. She devoted herself to good works, the Women's Institute, giving blood and I can particularly remember her selling pork pies from the kitchen window, though goodness knows why, because she certainly did not make them! Granny also bought up dishcloths made by someone in the village, because the whole family were kept supplied for years. Everyone remembered her on her sit-up-and-beg bike as she regularly cycled into Bedford until she was at least 80. She died in 1976 and is buried in the Monoux vault with my grandfather, on the left side of the graveyard as you go towards the church door. She bequeathed a very pretty little table to the church, which she attended twice on Sundays and always sat in the choir pews. I often hope that the table is still there, as sadly so much of value has been stolen from churches now. The family also gave the land for Wootton School to be built on.

My parents, Myra and Brian Wells, were married in Wootton Church and they owned Ivy Cottage for some years in the 1950's. I rang the church bells! Myself and my sisters all rode with Bill Juffs. My uncle, Derek Doyne-Ditmas farmed Manor Farm, Church Road in the 1940's and my aunt, Eyvor Pelham Reid, Wood Farm in the 40's to 60's. Sadly no members of the family now live anywhere close, but I come up on the train to the Record Office now and again."

Major Harold Edward Churton Doyne-Ditmas (1881-1945) and Sybil Harriet Monoux Payne (1885-1976) had seven children.

1. Eyvor Florence Sybil (1908-1999)
       married 1. Keane
                2. Reid
2. Nancy Ilean (1909-1999)
       married Abel
3. Myra Heather (1911-1989)
       married Wells
4. Philip Edward Churton Vigors (1918-1980)
       married 1. Turner
                2. Bower
5. Derek Harold Gordon Monoux (1919-1971)

married Fraser-Harris
6. Sybil Winifred Sheila (1923-)
married Eales-White
7. Harold Granville Terence Payne (1930-)
married 1. Davis
2. Edgeworth

Mrs Harfield's book "Major H.E.C. Doyne-Ditmas RFA, Grandfather's Footsteps" can be consulted at the Bedford Records Office and is a fascinating account of his life, both during the First World War and afterwards.

The Poor Law and Local Administration

As early as 1572, Parishes had to appoint Overseers or Collectors whose duties were the provision of Poor Relief for the sick and needy of the Parish. Their duties also included appointing Parish Constables who policed the village.

There are very few records surviving about Poor Relief in Wootton. There was a small Workhouse situated in Church Road, where the needy, sick and elderly could be housed. In the 1674 Hearth Tax returns, it was listed as having six hearths. The Overseers were appointed by the Parish annually. They were responsible for collecting money from each household according to its means and then during times of need or sickness, villagers could apply for financial help. The Overseers Accounts for the period 1784 to 1810 give a very good insight to the sorts of help, financial and otherwise, given. Elderly folk were supported by the Parish, sometimes in the Almshouses near the Church, or sometimes a family would be paid to have an elderly person as a lodger. For example in 1784 "Widow Christmas received six shillings a week". The records show that six or seven widows received help each week, rising to as many as 11 in 1798.

Wherever possible, families were expected to support their own dependents. In the case of illegitimate children, the Overseers would make strenuous attempts to find the father, persuading him to marry the girl or at least support the child. Orphans were often given to "baby farmers" to look after. In July 1794 "Beck Moore was paid 2/6 for Walkers Child". The Poor Law looked after pauper villagers from the cradle to the grave. In 1792, nine shillings and four pence was paid to Charles North for "a coffin and the fees for H. Curtis." At the same time, Mrs Emmerton, the local "layer out" was paid " eight shillings and eight pence halfpenny for two burials". Another "layer out", Eliza Watford, was paid "two shillings and sixpence, for laying out "Widow Fowkes". In 1792, Charles North charged "nine shillings and ten pence for Elizabeth Cowley's coffin."

Sometimes, relief took the form of food or clothing. In 1774, William Meese was "given one shilling to get his clothes out of pawn". John Hill, a local cobbler, was "paid seventeen shillings and three pence for shoes". "Four pairs of britches were bought for thirteen shillings and Sue Butcher was "paid two shillings for washing". Emergency payments were also made. In 1786 "two shillings and sixpence was given to Widow Rainbow who was in want".

To obtain relief from the Parish, the claimant had to prove they had "settlement" in that Parish. Overseers would only give help to their own villagers and would go to great lengths to avoid aiding other parishes' poor. In the notebooks of Samuel Whitbread, a local magistrate, he deals many times with men trying to prove which parish should support them. On Sunday October 10th, 1813, he heard a request from George Fuller from Henlow who wished to be examined as to his parish. George eventually came to live in Wootton. In 1814, John Johnson took his case to Whitbread, complaining that Wootton Parish had discontinued his allowance.

Magistrates would give judgement on all disputes between the Overseers and villagers. In 1814, Joseph Wadsworth from Wootton took two cases to Whitbread. He alleged he had not received wages for ditching from Nathaniel Cook and also made a claim against the Wootton Overseer, John Pateman, for relief as his wife was "infirm in her eyes". He was successful in obtaining the wages due and also had his

Mrs Russell, midwife and "layer out", taken outside of the backdoor of her cottage in Potters Cross (now demolished), opposite the Black Horse car park.

allowance increased to six shillings.

To feed the poor, food had to be purchased for the Workhouse. Wheat was bought at Bedford, then ground to make flour. Beans were bought in 1798 from Barnard Dimmock, a local farmer, for nineteen shillings. Occasionally a hog was bought and cost a shilling to kill. Cheese cost ten shillings and four pence and a quantity of beef was purchased one week "from Henry Haynes at two pence a pound". All in all, a very basic diet.

Where possible, the Overseers tried to supplement their income. In 1798, Mr Thompson, a local lace buyer, bought lace from the Overseers in Wootton and paid twenty-six pounds, nineteen shillings and two pence. The Overseers' fortnightly expenditure was between twenty and thirty pounds. However, in 1807, it reached over sixty pounds when there were 28 men and boys being financially helped. This must have been a time when jobs on the land were very scarce.

At the beginning of the 1800's, times were very hard in the rural areas. Jobs were scarce; Parish Overseers were finding it hard to meet all the claims for financial help. Marston, the next parish to Wootton, with a population of 1007, spent £2,082 in 1831. This was a national problem. There was an attempt to raise wages. Men were imprisoned for refusing to work for the normal wages prevailing. Riots broke out and there were cases of arson against the farmers who would not give a living wage. The Duke of Bedford's agent in November 1830, reported on a fire "at Benson's farm at Wootton Pillinge (now Stewartby) where all the buildings and the Brickyard were destroyed. Nothing saved but the farmhouse and the dovecote." The Agent, Mr Crocker continued to visit local vestries to persuade the farmers to employ more men. In December 1814 "there was a fire at Robinson's farm at Wootton Keeley between 12 and 1.00am." Some Parishes had schemes for setting the poor to work or helped families to emigrate to start a new life in the colonies. Some men "took the King's shilling" and joined the Army. Many years later, in the Bedfordshire Times, was reported the death of Richard Lambert, aged 84. He was a veteran of Waterloo and had obviously joined the Army, serving in the 14th Foot, leaving the village to enlist when work in Wootton became scarce in the early 1800's.

Eventually, in 1834, The Poor Law Act came into operation. Villages were formed into Poor Law Unions and Wootton became part of the Bedford Union. Boards of Guardians were elected and the Parish Overseers became responsible to them. The big problem was perceived to be "a surplus population in the rural areas". The solution was twofold, migration and emigration. Many went to the towns. Bedford, Luton and Dunstable grew during the mid 1800's. The Union at Bedford encouraged the unemployed men to seek work away from the land; many from the 1840's onwards went to work on the building of the railways. Many families moved to London and other big cities and, with the railways opening up the country migration was made easier.

Emigration too, could be paid for by the Union. In 1846, a Wootton man, William Parrott, transported to Norfolk Island as a convict, had the passage of his wife Mary and two children, paid for. Norfolk Island, 900 miles east of Sydney, Australia, was later to play host to some of the mutineers from the Bounty. The cost of a passage to Van Diemans Land in 1852, also part of Australia, was advertised at seven pounds, ten shillings for an adult and three pounds fifteen shillings for a child, considerably less than supporting a family through Poor Relief for a number of years. It took about four months to make the trip. 1851, the Bedford Union was finding it hard to obtain work locally for some of the girl inmates when they reached 12 years old. Girls, some from Wootton, were considered for positions in the colonies. Sending paupers to the colonies was by no means a new idea. As early as 1730 John Webb, aged 16, was indentured for four years to John Taylor and sent to work in Jamaica, on the plantations.

The type of work undertaken by the paupers at the Workhouse at Bedford included gardening by the old men, grinding of corn by hand mills by the able bodied men, women undertook washing, sewing and household duties, boys would do tailoring, shoe making, baking bread and gardening, girls knitted, sewed and also undertook duties. Only the old ladies were allowed to escape any jobs at all. The Workhouse was in Bedford, where South Wing Hospital now stands. Aged and infirm, the sick and lunatics became the responsibility of the Union and all the villages paid towards the costs.

In 1840, Bedfordshire had the makings of a Police force beginning under the guidance of the new Chief Constable, Captain Boultbee. At first, the Constables were unpopular but eventually they took over the policing from the Overseers' constables. In 1841, the local paper, the Mercury was very concerned at the cost of rural policing, it had risen to over three thousand pounds a year. However, in the same edition it congratulated the police in their detection of a burglary at Newport Pagnell when £30 of goods were stolen. The thieves were all caught, most of the property recovered and all four of the prisoners dealt with by the Buckinghamshire magistrates. Thomas Williamson, aged 19, living in Newport Pagnell but born and brought up in Keeley Lane, Wootton, was transported for 15 years to Tasmania. Sentences were indeed severe, many men resorted to sheep stealing or poaching, simply to put a meal on the table, regardless of the severe punishments inflicted if caught.

The Police made use of the old Lockups in the rural areas. These cages or buildings were used by the Parishes to house vagrants as well as the Police prisoners. The one in Wootton used to stand on land belonging to Wootton House, just outside the churchyard walls. The Overseers also had a pound where stray animals were collected. The one in Wootton was repaired in 1863 by Sir Coventry Payne and stood on the land next to the telephone kiosk in the Bedford Road, opposite the Cock Inn. Eventually, police houses were built with their own cells for prisoners.

Education

Sunday Schools

Early education had its beginnings in Sunday Schools, both Anglican and Non Conformist, which often led to competition. As early as 1611, soon after the Authorised Version of the Bible was published, there was a Puritan school in Wootton for teaching bible study in peoples' own language. Teachers could be licensed by the Bishop "as a suitable man for his calling", but in 1617, a Mr Smythe was teaching in a school in Wootton without a licence. In 1717, the Vicar of Wootton reported to the Bishop of Lincoln, that there was a public school in Wootton, "the number of children in it is sometimes more, sometimes less. They are taught the Church catechism and they come to church". The formation of the Bedfordshire Institution of 1815 allowed the Church of England to instruct in any kind of education with the principles of the Church of England. This seems to have been abandoned by 1830 and there appeared to be hardly any schools, or only a few of a very low standard in Bedfordshire. An attribute to this was the need for child labour to aid the rural economy.

Lace Schools

Some villages had a lace school; often the only school in the village where girls started from the ages of 3-5 and Wootton was no exception. The schools gave scarcely any formal education and were often just sweat shops. One such lace school in Wootton was situated near Keeley Corner. The nearby village of Marston Moretaine was known to have nine lace making schools so it is extremely likely that nearby Wootton would have had more than one. The lace schools started each morning with a reading from the Bible and that was all the schooling given. Such lace schools are recorded as early as 1785. There are references to them in the Overseers Accounts, and links to Mr Barnard Dimmock, a local farmer, one of the Overseers, who also had a connection with the Church. In an agricultural area such as Wootton, the income from children and women's lace making was a very important addition to the family budget indeed. In the 1851 census, the main occupation for men in Wootton (over 70%) was that of agricultural labourer and a very high proportion of their wives (almost 50%), gave their occupation as "lace making".

National Surveys into Local Education Provision

Thomas Gadsby, the Vicar of Wootton, wrote in 1818 that Wootton had a population of 831. There were no particulars of any money relating to the education of children and no schools. The Parish had no means of supplying a fund to educate the poor. Between 1818 and 1833 there was an improvement in the provision of elementary education. On the King's instruction, the Home Secretary, Melbourne sent out a questionnaire to the Overseers of the Poor in all Parishes asking about the existence of Day and Sunday Schools.

In 1833, the information from Wootton was: - "population 1051, one Daily School commenced 1824 containing 20 males and 10 females belonging to the Baptists. 30 males and 30 females in the Baptist Sunday School. A Sunday School supported by T. Gadsby, Vicar with 57 males and 53 females with a salary paid by the Vicar of £4. In the Methodist Sunday School 40 males and 60 females. The teacher in these Sunday Schools gave their services gratuitously".

As a result of the obvious need for education provision throughout the nation, Government Grants were started for National Schools from 1834-1838.

In 1844 a Church of England Inspector, Rev. John Allen, said of Wootton: - population 1,122. "The endowed school kept in a poor room under an inefficient master. Hope of a new room being built soon."

In 1847 The Church School Inquiry said of Wootton "Sunday School 58 boys, 50 girls. No Daily School. A school would be a great benefit to the Parish. A room for a Sunday School is wanted, the school is now being held in the Church." This enquiry was for Church of England schools only.

The first school was built in 1860 on a site in Bedford Road, where the four Georgian style houses are now, next to the Cock Inn. It was a Church School, eventually becoming the Infants School.

Dame Schools

There was a possibility that Wootton had some Dame Schools. In the Beds Times on the 5th January 1855, there was an advert: - "The Misses Cooper respectfully inform their friends that their pupils will re-assemble on Tuesday January 23rd. Terms and references forwarded on application". This could have been Eliza Cooper, a Governess, born in Ampthill in 1830, and who, in 1851 was the Governess to the children in Grey Lodge, next to the Methodist Church.

1870 Education Act

The 1870 Education Act involved a careful Parish by Parish examination of existing elementary education provision. It took two years to complete. When the Education Department had reached its conclusion, printed details were sent to every Parish to be published. In the Bedfordshire Mercury during July and August 1872, it said of Wootton "Existing, no efficient School. Required accommodation for 150 boys and girls and 100 infants in Wootton village."

The Minutes of the School stated on November 26th 1874, "Proposed by Mr Paine and seconded by Mr W. F. Redman that a Committee of three ratepayers of the parish to be appointed to confer with the Trustees of the present school and obtain their intentions with regard to the future conduct of the same. Committee as follows: - W. F. Swaffield, G. Line, B. Dimmock."

The Minutes of the 8th December 1874 read "The Vicar of Wootton ascertained that they were quite willing that it should continue to be carried on as the school for the Parish with any enlargement of which it might be capable but that from the nature of the trust they could not make any formal transfer of it to the Parish. A letter was to be sent to the Education Department that nothing has changed to increase the school accommodation in this Parish".

A final notice was issued in the Mercury on 31st January 1875. "Existing no efficient school. Required accommodation for 150 boys and girls and 100 infants. Wootton Church of England School can be made efficient for 148 children."

The First Board School

The Wootton Board School was built in 1877, by Sir Philip Payne, the local Lord of the Manor. The account in the Bedford Mercury of 7th April 1877 reads "On Tuesday last the foundation stone was laid at the above place (Wootton) for a new Public Elementary School. The weather was not very favourable for the occasion, but still about the time appointed for the stone to be laid the rain had somewhat subsided; all the arrangements for this auspicious occasion were excellently set forth upon a printed programme. The building is situated in the midst of the village, some 50 to 100 yards from St. Mary's School, and placed beside the high road leading to Bedford. The erection of the school was offered for public competition and Messrs. Long and Potter were the successful candidates, the price they

The view along the Bedford Road looking towards Bedford. On the right is the Infants School, built in 1860.

The Old School showing the School House on the right. It was built in 1877 on the corner of Bedford Road and Church Road.

offered in the tender being £1,442. The architecture of the school is plain, and apparently it will be a very commodious building, the dimensions of the large room being 54 feet by 20 feet. The inhabitants were greatly opposed to the erection of the school at first as they thought the village school was sufficient to meet the requirements of their children".

The first schoolmaster was Mr William Henry Mepham and he recorded that "in December 1879, Lizzie Mepham, formerly Garrett, his wife, qualified as a teacher after doing her probation at Wootton Board School". The school was inspected in December 1883 and it was noted "that Mr Mepham was improving the school". The inspections each year following showed a steady improvement with comments in 1888 that "the elementary work has gained in accuracy" and in 1889 "this improvement continued" although in 1886, teachers were said to "be hampered by poor attendance".

When the Bedfordshire Archiodiconal Board for Education took over, more money was given to encourage school building in the County. By the end of the 1890's there was a big move to School Boards. A village School Board comprised of five people elected from among the ratepayers and they held office for three years. This meant the Board could be dominated by one group. In Wootton, there were long periods of non-conformist control.

In the 1876 Education Act, School Attendance Committees were formed. Bedfordshire had six. In 1903, the Bedfordshire Education Committee was established and School Boards were abolished. On 30th September 1903, all Board Schools became Council Schools. The Authority became responsible for secular education and payment of teachers and the general running of the schools.

In 1876, education became compulsory and when Balfour passed his Act in 1902, education became the responsibility of local authorities. In 1906 the School Meals Service began, and in 1907 scholarships for poor children to Grammar Schools started.

The old St. Mary's School was used by the Sunday School, as a Parish Room and as an annexe to the Infants School. At one time Primary Education in the village was on four sites, two classes in St. Mary's Church School, a class of infants at the Baptist Chapel, the Board School had three classes of Seniors and the old church hall by the vicarage was used for school meals.

Pupil Teachers

To obtain enough teachers, able pupils were made monitors or pupil teachers for four years under the direction of the Head Teacher. This was a form of apprenticeship. This type of training went on into the beginning of the 20th century. Teachers began training at 13 and when 18, could sit an examination for the Queen's Scholarship and then enter Training College

School group in 1922, with Mr Talbot, Headmaster.

Back row (LEFT TO RIGHT): Fred Lowe, Bill Moore, Walter Cooper, Stan Lovell, Reg Lowe, Reg Ellis.

Second row (LEFT TO RIGHT): Doris Russell, Alice Milton, Winnie Curtis, Alice Baker, Molly Mead, Olive Lambert, Phyllis Whitbread, Nellie Hutchings, Lou Lowe, Mr Talbot.

Third row (LEFT TO RIGHT): Lizzie Cooper, Maud Robinson, Lily Tysoe, Winnie Lowe, ? Fuller, Connie Sanders, Mabel Cornish.

Bottom row (LEFT TO RIGHT): Ern Gilbert, Ted Lovell, Reg Manyweathers, Sid Caves, Alf Curtis.

Connie Sanders later became a teacher at Wootton School herself.

Mr Frank Crisp, Headmaster of Wootton School, with the top form of 1954.

Back row (LEFT TO RIGHT): Malcolm Peddar, Trevor Bavington, Robin Stafferton, Terry Goff, Peter Caves, David Williamson.

Third row (LEFT TO RIGHT): Graham Robinson, Mary Trussell, Barbara Burraway, Anne Freestone, Dawn Heath, Melvyn Sharpe.

Second row (LEFT TO RIGHT): Jean Bryant, Pat Egan, Doreen Walton, Mr Frank Crisp, Anita Lovell, Margaret Hutchings, Valerie Shaw.

Front row (LEFT TO RIGHT): Susan Attrill, Jean Burraway, Janice Burraway.

with a Government Grant. In Wootton, an example of this type of training was undertaken by Constance Mary Robinson (nee Sanders). She left school at 14 after passing her Monitor examination. She then took her Pupil Teacher examination, and having passed, went on to attend Queens Park School for training on Saturdays. Whilst teaching, Connie passed her examination for the certificate in 1927, with credits in Arithmetic and Music. She did a supply apprenticeship of 12 months, cycling to the villages of Dean, Dunstable, Keysoe, Eastcotts, Cranfield and Marston, staying the whole week and returning to Wootton at weekends.

After all this training, Connie applied and was accepted for a vacancy, at Wootton Primary School. Connie herself, had attended the Church School when Mr and Mrs Talbot were Head Teachers and it was they who encouraged Connie to take up teaching. She taught the seven and eight year olds and had about 40 children in her class.

Children moved around little in those days, sitting for most lessons, in high desks. They had inkwells in the desks but also used chalkboards, slates and slate pencils. Learning by rote was the norm, tables were recited out loud. Reading was regarded with importance and much time was spent learning to read. There were few books and most work had to be copied from the board. This system lasted well into the 1950's.

Secondary Education

Stewartby School, the present Marston Vale Middle School, opened on 26th October 1935. It was intended just before the Second World War, that children at age 11 years would transfer to a secondary school. Up to that point, village schools were known as "all age schools" and catered for children of five up to school leaving age of 14, and then 15. Some children did cycle, at age 11, to Stewartby just before the War, but this was considered too dangerous once war broke out, and Wootton children (if they had a bike!) did not start to attend the Stewartby School until 1946. Eventually a bus was provided and then all children went. The passing of the 11 plus allowed youngsters from Wootton to go to Harpur Trust Schools in Bedford or Stratton School. There had always been Scholarships available to the Harpur Trust Schools, even before the 11 plus was introduced.

The Lower School

The present Lower School opened in 1962, taking children up to the age of 11. However, when Bedfordshire adopted a three-tier system, it

Celebration Teas held on May 6th 1910, to mark the accession to the throne of King George V. In the Background is the Old School.

Fancy Dress to celebrate the Coronation in 1937. "King" Arthur Curtis and "Queen" Vivienne Attrill. Other children: K. Hutchings, S. Hutchings, D. Haynes, N. Beard, P. Freestone, G. Moore, K. Russell, C. Pateman, F. Bennett, B. Caves, J. Hutchings, A. Burraway, M. Baxter, P. Watford, B. Biggs, P. Keep, R. Hutchings, B. Tysoe, M. Ashpole, P. Loft.

became a Lower School and Wootton children at age nine, went mainly to Holywell Middle School, Cranfield. Now there is more choice, and village children may opt for one of the other local Middle Schools.

History of Wootton Upper School

Wootton Upper School started in 1975. As the school buildings were not quite ready, it shared a site with Stewartby Middle School. The first intake was 213 students and they moved onto the Wootton site in the November, with 16 teaching staff. The first Headmaster was Mr Stanley Clews, with Deputy Head, Mr John Popplewell. The school was complete by 1978. Mr Clews retired in 1987 and then Mrs Catherine Mackenzie took over until 1999. The present Head is Mr Anthony Withell. The Upper School catchment area covers far more villages than just Wootton and having achieved Beacon Status in 2001; it is regarded as one of the top Upper Schools in the County.

Churches of Wootton

The Ecclesiastical Census

This Census of Church Membership was taken on March 30th 1851 throughout England. At that time, the population of Wootton was recorded as 1,204 and the details of the three Churches established in the village at that time shows the size of their membership.

St. Mary's Parish Church, Anglican

General Congregation:
Morning 150
Afternoon 380
Sunday School 100
Jas. Jenkyn, Vicar.

Particular Baptist, 1836

'Country Congregations in Agricultural districts are always fluctuating. Much depends on the weather, the seasons of the year, the diversified sate of respective families. Some can only attend at one part of the day, others twice and some few on every public service. Therefore, I give the same return here that I usually make in our denominational returns. The general number that attend my ministry is from one to two hundred.'

William Early, Pastor.

Wesleyan Methodist, 1811

General Congregation:
Morning 46
Afternoon 99
Evening 140
Sunday School 100
Charles Armstrong, Society Steward

No Catholic Congregation was recorded. Church and Chapel attendance in Wootton that Sunday was at least 780 adults and children out of a population of 1204 recorded in the population census that year, almost 65% of the village.

St. Mary's Parish Church, Wootton

Many churches were built in the 12th century and Wootton Church dates from this period. Simon de Beauchamp bestowed the Church in Wootton on Newnham Priory in his Foundation Charter around 1166 and in 1224, Hugh of Wells, Bishop of Lincoln, confirmed the appropriation of the Church. The ordination of the Vicarage by the Bishop of Gravesend took place in 1272. There is a continuous list of the Vicars of Wootton from 1258 (see Appendix 10). The Parish Priest was one of the few people in the village who could read and write and most of the services would be said or sung in Latin. There would be few seats and most of the congregation stood during the long services.

The bare white walls would have been covered with colourful murals depicting saints and biblical scenes, which were used as visual aids for an illiterate population.

The priest did much to help the poor and the church was supported by Tithes, the biblical principle of giving one tenth of income or produce to the Church. Certain bequests to the Parish of land, houses and money, form the basis of the Wootton Charities. Income from these too, was used to support the poor and also help repair the fabric of the Church. In the early 1800's, the Wootton Charities owned, amongst other property, two cottages in Cause End, three in Hall End, a house and farm buildings in Church Road as well as a number of fields. By 1847, the Trustees had eventually sold the cottages and most of the lands and the money was invested to provide an annual income for the Charity as it still does today.

The church was rebuilt in the early 14th century, the tower and the south porch being added later. After the Reformation, when Henry VIII broke away from Rome, an English translation of the Bible was placed in the Church, but few could read it.

During the time of Cromwell, any statues and decorations were removed from churches and painted walls were covered with white plaster.

By the 16th Century, the Church was in need of restoration and eventually the rectory and the patronage of the church became the possession of Humphrey Monoux and stayed with the family until the beginning of the 19th century. In the Chancel, there are memorials and tablets to the Monoux and Payne families. The earliest is to Lt. Philip Monoux, who was slain in the service of the King (James II) whilst fighting the rebels of the late Duke of Monmouth, in Somerset on June 19th 1685, in the 29th year of his life.

Some restoration work was carried out but the church was in much need of repair when the Reverend Neale became Vicar in 1852. Under his direction and with much of the work completed at his own personal cost, the church was restored about 1860.

After Neale's death in 1872, further improvements were carried out by his successors. The organ was restored and improved for the Diamond Jubilee of Queen Victoria. Recent works carried out since 1959 include the re-leading of the spire, organ repairs, and a new roof covering on the nave and aisles. The most recent improvements were to the west end of the church in 1995.

The first impression when entering the church is one of height and space. The arcades are tall and date from the re-building of the church in the decorated style. Below the chancel arch is the 15th century screen. The south doorway dates from the 14th century and leads into a 14th century stone porch. The windows of the chancel are decorated in style. The stained glass of the window was inserted in 1890 in memory of the infant son of Sir Philip Monoux Payne. In the north wall of the chancel is a restored 14th century window with the glass in memory of Charles Henry Dillon who died in 1901. The upper part of the tower is early 15th century work; the lower part has largely been re-built. When the spire was restored in 1959, a lead panel bearing the names of William Emmerton and William Russell, former bell founders of Wootton was discovered.

The entrance to the tower is in the new choir vestry and there are six bells. Both the second and fourth bells were cast at Wootton, at a foundry about 200 yards from the Church, along Cause End Road. Thomas Russell began casting about 1710 and was later followed by his sons Thomas and William. Thomas Russell the elder, died in 1744 and the foundry closed. It was re-opened in 1767 by William Emmerton and closed again in 1790.

St. Mary's has always played a leading role in the social life of the village. In the early years, Sunday was often the only non working day for most villagers and the various churches and chapels in Wootton provided much of the social life. Fetes, concerts, picnics and so on, feature every week in the accounts of Wootton life in the local papers from Victorian times onwards. Reverend A. J. Foster M.A., started St. Mary's own Parish Magazine in 1882 with accounts of all the church activities.

Today the elaborate services are things of the past and since 1980, most services are in modern and up to date language. Wootton is a thriving church today. As well as the regular services, there are meetings for all age groups, including activities for children and young people. In Wootton the various denominations work together with united services and other events.

(top)

This view of St. Mary's Parish Church which hangs in the vestry, was drawn in pencil in 1854 and then colour washed, by the local Bedford architect and surveyor, John Sunman Austin, 1806-1860. He was quite an eccentric character, spending time in Bedford Lunatic Asylum and twice in Bedford Prison for debt, in 1846 and 1853, finally dying in Oxford in 1860. Having been widowed and left with six children to support, he eked out a living, doing architectural drawings of local buildings.

(left)

The gravestone of William Early, first Pastor and founder of the Baptist Church in Wootton. The graveyard of the Baptist Church now forms part of the car park.

The Baptist Church

William Early was born in Winchester in 1774 and moved into the area from Lockerley in Hampshire. From October 1824 to May 1825 he pastored the Baptist Church at Cranfield before moving to Wootton, with his wife Mary.

A printer by trade, Mr Early opened a day school in his home in Cause End Road, Wootton (now called Yew Tree Cottage). Protestant dissenters had been meeting for religious worship at various homes in the village since 1808, but a further application was made in February 1826 to worship in the house of William Early, supported by Joseph Caves, James Negus, Henry Hekks, Joshua Hull and J. Mays. According to the early minute book, William Early received a unanimous call from his small congregation to become their pastor, which he accepted and "entered upon it's duties" in October 1826.

As the church began to increase in membership Rev. Early sought to acquire a more suitable building for the meetings of the new Baptist Cause. In 1836, in conjunction with John Lovell, mealman, Richard Early, grocer, Samuel Lovell, shopkeeper, Henry Hekks, husbandman, Jonathan Lambert, husbandman, James Redman, wheelwright, William Redman, the elder, farmer, William Redman, the younger, builder, Thomas Redman, farmer, William Whitehouse, baker, Joseph Whitehouse, farmer, William Harris, the younger, farmer, William Moore, carpenter, William Vincent, the elder, general dealer, James Furr, husbandman and Charles Summerfield, husbandman, a parcel of land containing 15 poles "being part of a certain close called Beards Close" in High Street (now Bedford Road) Wootton was purchased from John Berry for the sum of 18 pounds and 15 shillings. A Church or Meeting House was built and opened for the worship of Almighty God in March 1836 at a cost of £400.

Rev. William Early resigned the pastorate in 1852, after serving the Church for 27 years. He preached his farewell sermon on Sunday 14th March from 2Corinthians 13 v11. He died 5th April 1853 aged 79 years and was buried in the chapel burial ground with his wife Mary, who had died on 19th November 1848, from typhus fever. A tablet to his memory is in the church.

In 1853 funds were raised to build a house adjoining the chapel, for the minister to reside in, at a cost of £120. When the house was demolished in 1994 a stone jar was discovered in the cavity, containing documents from William Early's replacement, a pastor Thomas Smith, and a list of names of contributors to its erection.

The chapel was extended further in the 1950's when they received the gift of a piece of land from Mrs Doyne-Ditmas, allowing a good sized school room to be added. In 1976 this was extended a second time and the church now enjoys a very large schoolroom, kitchen, toilets and meeting rooms.

After the Registration Act of 1836 couples were allowed to marry in non-conformist churches as well as the Established Church, which had previously reserved the right to perform all marriages. Wootton Baptist Church was registered, so being allowed to perform marriages on August 10th 1855 and village people could now choose where they were married. Paul Betny, writing in 1860 about village life, records in his book, "Rambles in Bedfordshire"; "Dissenting places are now licensed to convert two persons into one, folks have their choice of place, according to conscience, in which to plight their troth and take each other for better or worse, as the case may be according to their means or inclination, or of both and can choose whom they please to forge the chain of Hymen, from a Bishop down to a grimy blacksmith of Gretna Green notoriety. And so it turned out that on Friday 11th November last, the villagers of Wootton were incited to much gossip at witnessing the wedding of the second couple who had the temerity to depart from the time-honoured rule and to have this ceremony performed in the Baptist meeting-house." Further research has revealed that the couple getting married on this occasion were in fact William Lambert aged 21 years, tilemaker, son of Jonathan Lambert and Betsy Benson aged 20 years, daughter of Thomas Benson. Both were residents of Wootton.

And so the chapel continued to play an important role in the village, involving many people through the very large Sunday School, Sunday

Sunday School Outing from the Baptist Church in 1925 to Wickstead Park, Kettering.

Back row (LEFT TO RIGHT):
Elsie Faulkner (Lambert), Alice Denton (Frear), Jess Lovell (Denton), Elsie Lowe (Brooks), Alice Lovell (Tory).

Front row (LEFT TO RIGHT):
Gladys Beard, Bill Faulkner.

Marriage of Kate Mary Pope, aged 23, daughter of John Pope, shoemaker and clerk to Wootton Parish Council, and Ernest John Webster, aged 22, son of James Webster, a cowman. The marriage took place at the Baptist Chapel, 7th September 1898.

Front row:

Centre, Mrs Mary Pope, Bride, Kate Mary Pope, children, Leonard James Walker, Jessie Louise Walker, children of Robert and Elizabeth Walker.

Middle row
(RIGHT TO LEFT):

Robert John Walker, Elizabeth Walker (nee Pope), who were themselves married at the Baptist Chapel, 11th November 1880, Sarah Pope, Ernest John Webster (bridegroom), ?, Harriet Pope (wife of John), Ruth Pope (John's unmarried sister), John Pope (born 1848, died 7th June 1923).

Back row:

2nd from right, Jane Pope, Centre, Jesse Lambert.

Services and midweek meetings. Special services such as Sunday School anniversaries, Church anniversaries and harvest festivals were always very well attended and sit-down teas were a "must" for every occasion. The Bedford Mercury newspaper of 20th September 1881 reports, "On Sunday last the anniversary services of Wootton Baptist Sunday School were held and three sermons were preached by Mr. T. Cook of Luton. The congregations were good throughout the day, but in the evening the congregation was so large that many were unable to get inside the chapel."

Anniversaries were always followed with a fun day for the children and again the Bedford Mercury for September 1882 reports: "Following the Sunday School anniversary a delighted party went in wagons to Mr. Burr's farm at Kempston West End. Over 100 children sat down to tea first, then 90 friends. For the pleasure of the youngsters, swings, a see-saw and a greasy pole had been put up."

Every August bank holiday a Sunday School treat was held in a field where the Blue Cross Football Club now stands, the entrance to it being where the gateway of 58 Bedford Road is. There were games, races and swings for everyone followed by tea. Later on in the early part of the 1900's outings were arranged to Wickstead Park in charabancs and as transport became more readily available, to the seaside.

The chapel still has a thriving congregation today and remains faithful to its original trust deed of 1836, being a witness to God in the village.

Methodism in Wootton

The Wesleyans were apparently the first Free Church to hold properly organised meetings to worship as their conscience dictated and a licence to worship in that manner was applied for in the name of Daniel Cooke to be held in his house in March 1806. The certificate was again applied for in the name of Samuel Sheffield in April 1807 and again in 1810 from the house of John Vaux and additionally John Curtis, Thomas Warren, John Thomas and Daniel Cooke.

In 1811 two cottages were purchased and adapted for church

purposes, they were opened for worship in August of the same year. John Curtis the younger of Wootton, lace dealer and John Dowsett of St. Cuthberts, Bedford, surgeon and apothecary bought the piece of land 57 feet in length by 24 feet in breadth at Church End, Wootton, along with the two cottages, from a shopkeeper, Ambrose Hurst, for the sum of £80, payable in two payments of £40. Samuel Corby and William Estick, labourers, had been the previous tenants. The first payment of £40 was paid on 18th April 1811.

On 6th January 1812, a conveyance and trust deed was made giving effect to the purchase and the following came in as Trustees, when the second payment was paid.

John Curtis	of Wootton	Lace dealer
Daniel Cook	of Wootton	Farmer
John Dowsett	of St. Cuthberts, Bedford	Surgeon
Richard Lovell	of St. Peters, Bedford	Shoemaker
John Maynard	of St. Peters, Bedford	Wheelwright
Isaac Wale	of St. Pauls, Bedford	Tailor
John Issett	of St. Pauls, Bedford	Butcher
William Cumberland	of St. Marys, Bedford	Shoemaker
William Yates	of Kempston	Farmer

The terms of the trust were given agreeing that the use of the chapel should be for the purpose of preaching and expanding God's Holy Word. If doctrines, conducts or abilities of any preacher were thought to be erroneous immoral or deficient, then the Trustees would proceed according to the Rules of Pacification laid down in the Conference of Methodist minutes of 1795.

New Trustees were appointed in February 1840 on the deaths of John Curtis, Daniel Cook, Richard Lovell, William Cumberland and William Yates namely:

| Rev. Maximillian Wilson | of Bedford | Wesleyan Minister |
| Rev. Thomas Poulton-Clark | of Ampthill | Wesleyan Minister |

Family photograph of the Keep family, bakers of Hall End, taken in 1898.

Left to right: Annie, Thomas, John, Emma, Sarah, Hettie (Henrietta).

Thomas started as a shoemaker, but then founded a bakery in Hall End, in two of the cottages opposite the Chequers Pub. Annie married Walter Swannell of the Ampthill Bakery. Henrietta married his brother, Bert, an insurance man. Sarah married Walter Fardell, also a baker, from opposite the Memorial Hall. Thomas was also a Wesleyan Lay Preacher. He passed the bakery on to his son, Richard.

Charles Armstrong	of Wootton	Farmer
Samuel Warren	of Wootton	Collar Maker
James Hebbes	of Wootton	Brickmaker
James Summerfield	of Wootton	Labourer
William Furr	of Wootton	Labourer

The Church was described by Paul Betney in his book "Rambles in Bedfordshire", 1860, as an "Oblong shape. The interior was neat, clean and commodious and gathers numerous congregations of worshippers twice on Sundays and one evening each week".

On January 1st 1862 at a quarterly meeting of the Bedford Circuit, which included the whole of Bedford, Ampthill and the churches of numerous villages in and around Bedford it was unanimously agreed that a piece of land be purchased suitable for the erection of a new chapel and schoolroom. The site chosen belonged to the Armstrong family who generously donated £100 towards the project, as did Mr John Howard of Bedford.

The corner stone was laid on July 22nd 1862; the total cost being £330-16s-6d, and was opened on 6th February 1863.

The chapel was registered for the solemnising of marriages on August 3rd 1895 and 1911 land was acquired for the erection of a pastor's house.

The chapel was extensively altered in 1964 providing additional amenities.

Bedford Mercury, 14th February 1863, Wootton

Opening of the Wesleyan Chapel and School. The beautiful and commodious edifice recently erected for the Wesleyan body at this place was opened on the 6th inst., when the Rev. Rattenbury, ex-President of the Wesleyan Conference, preached two eloquent sermons on behalf of the chapel fund, - in the afternoon and evening. The chapel was inconveniently crowded on each occasion. Between the two services about 200 persons sat down and partook of an excellent tea, in the new

Schoolroom.

On the Friday following, the Rev. S. Waddy D.D., also preached two sermons on behalf of the chapel fund.

Wootton at Work

Brick Making

Wootton is built on the Oxford Clay belt and as a result, the making of bricks and tiles has long provided work for the men of the area. One of the earliest references to brick making is in the Parish Registers when the burial of the wife of William Witt, a brick maker took place in 1681, followed the next year by the burial of William himself, who was then described as a tile burner. Thomas Berry and Thomas Brown, both called brick makers, were buried in 1771 and 1774. In the Survey of Bedfordshire published in 1979 by Bedfordshire County Council, references are made to four known brick kilns. The oldest was a brick and tile kiln at Wood End, referred to in 1655, 1687 and 1727. "Brick Yard Kilns" and "Kiln Pits" appear as field names in the Enclosure Map of 1838. It is known that this site was operated by John North between 1727 and 1737.

Another brickfield was in operation near to Tinkers Corner by at least 1865. It operated until 1916 and no doubt some of the distinctive yellowish bricks visible in the cottages at this corner of Wootton are from this kiln. It was owned by the Payne family, the Lords of the Manor, and worked by Thomas Dudley, succeeded by John Dudley in about 1885. Sir Philip Payne himself took over the management by 1903, running it until it closed. Under him, there were six kilns and three men employed.

To the north west of Keeley Lane was a third kiln, operating definitely by 1854 and shown also on the Enclosure Map of 1838. Working until 1898 and run by the Hebbes family, firstly by Charles Hebbes senior and then his son, also Charles. They also operated kilns at Kempston and Wilstead. The kilns had been pulled down by 1901.

Finally, there was a brickworks to the south of Fields Road, opened in 1901 and disused by 1914. It was operated by Caleb Summerfield (after whom, Summerfield Drive is named) and his son James. James was also licensee of the Rose and Crown Public House, Keeley Green.

A group of workers of the original Wootton Pillinge Brick and Tile Company, taken at Kimberly (the old brick kiln), between 1908 and 1910.

Back row (LEFT TO RIGHT): C. Lambert, ?, Archie Moore, ?, Fred Milton, Sam Robinson, Arthur Beard, ?, Joe Granby, V. Haddow, ?, ?, Baker.

Standing fourth row (LEFT TO RIGHT): Walt Lowe, Jack Stapleton, Brown, ?, ?, ?, F. Moore, ?, ?, ?, Eric Ashpole, George Harris, ?, ?, Toby Crowsley, ?.

Standing third row (LEFT TO RIGHT): John Robinson, Tom Parrott, Jonty Farrer, Ernie Turvey, Wright, Robinson, ?, Fred Tuffnell, ?, ?, G. Moore, ?, ?, ?.

Seated on chairs (LEFT TO RIGHT): H. Moore, ?, ?, Mr Neill, ?, ?, ?, Sam Baker.

Seated on ground (LEFT TO RIGHT): H. Robinson, F. Baker, Ellis, Folkes, ?, ?, ?, Jesse Moore, Albie Gilbert.

The occupation of brick making continued to be the mainstay of the economy of Wootton until well into the twentieth century. By this time, the brick works were situated along the Marston Valley and men from the village would walk or cycle to them each day. The village of Stewartby, originally part of the parish known as Wootton Pillinge, became a separate civil parish in 1937. Bricks had been made in that area since 1898. During the First World War, the works became almost derelict but by 1926 it had expanded greatly and employed over 500 men. Although there had been two blocks of four cottages built as early as 1910 for the workers, the main development of the present village of Stewartby began in 1926. Sid Cook's elder sister was one of the first to move in there with her husband and Sid can remember going to stay there as a small child. He felt it was just like a real holiday with running hot water in the houses and indoor flush toilets!

Clocks, Bells and Watch Makers

Thomas Russell was born in Hampshire in 1667, apprenticed as a watch and clockmaker to Thomas Merryman in London, married in London in 1697 and arrived in Wootton in 1700. As well as an excellent clock maker, examples can still be seen at Luton and Bury St. Edmunds' Museums, he took up bellfounding in about 1710, his earliest surviving bell being one at Melchborne dated 1712. The site of the bell foundry is in Cause End Road at Astra House (formerly the Star Inn). Thomas died in January 1744/45 and the work was carried on by firstly his son, also Thomas, and then his brother, William. On his death, the business was taken over by William Emmerton, a former apprentice to William Russell. Emmerton cast some 33 known bells between 1768 and 1789, including complete rings of five for Tilsworth (1776) and Bedford St. John (1786) and six for Biddenham (1787). Emmerton died in 1789, owning land in Ridgmont and in Bott End, Wootton. His son, who had taken over a business in Woburn, died just four years later and was also buried at Wootton. Another member of the Emmerton family also worked in Olney.

The horse and cart, belonging to the Wiles family, delivering milk. At one time, there were three dairies serving the village.

Harvest time on Wiles Farm. Taken about 1950 in the rick-yard at Tinkers Corner, it shows how many workers were needed at harvest time. In the photo are three generations of the Wiles family.

Back: Alan Clark
Standing (LEFT TO RIGHT): William Wiles (Bill), David Wiles, Joe Osborne, William Burraway (Bill), Michael Wiles, Albert Wiles, Clive Wiles, Richard Wiles (Dick).
Seated (LEFT TO RIGHT): Roland Wiles, Albert Charles Wiles.

Albert Charles Wiles was the farm Manager for Sir Arthur Black before going into partnership with Joe Osborne.

Agriculture

Work on the land provided most families with their living up to the end of the 1800's. Until the coming of machinery, all tasks on a farm would be undertaken by manpower. Horses were the other main source of power and the ancillary trades of blacksmith and wheelwright flourished well into the 20th century. The blacksmiths shop stood where Wootton garage now is. Mechanical vehicles started to appear in the first part of the 1900's. Sid Cook remembers one of the first cars in the village, a Ruby 7, belonging to an Insurance agent who lived in the Bedford Road. Sid also remembered as a small boy, taking the battery that ran the household's radio into the Garage for re-charging and collecting it after school the same day. As the batteries stood on the bench being re-charged, the Garage resounded with the sound of all the batteries "ticking" away.

All of the fields in the village had their own particular names. Examples are Kiln Wood, which lay between Hall End corner and the wood with Brakelands next to it. Tippings was the field in Hall End, where the searchlight battery was based in World War II. Jonties was the next field to the cemetery and Fisher's Field lay between Cause End Road to Hall End.

In the early 1900's the wheelwrights at Keeley Corner was in operation. It was run by the Redman family, who were also carpenters and undertakers. It had been established by Ciceley McKeegan's great grandfather, John. Wheels for farm carts and other vehicles were still made of wood until well into the mid 1900's. The "tyres" were iron, heated until red hot and placed on the wooden rim and then rapidly cooled with cold water, to shrink the iron on tightly. This was always an exciting and dramatic sight and sound for any youngsters watching. John Redman had a secondary occupation of undertaking, employing a lady to "lay out" the deceased. The family made the coffins and kept the bier in the bier house in the churchyard. John's son, then followed by his three sons, all went into the family business. They felled their own trees, cut them into planks, then seasoned them for seven years. The business also made and decorated carts. In 1948, fire destroyed the firm, and not being fully

73

insured, the three brothers had to seek alternative employment. Lewis moved to Marston but Robert and Archie continued living at Keeley Corner.

Lace Making

The production of Bedfordshire lace played a large part in the lives of local women. There is a record of lace being bought from the Wootton Overseers by Richard Stimpson, a lace buyer from Wootton, in 1784 and 1788. All through the census returns for the 19th century, the second most common occupation after that of agricultural labourer, was lace maker. The income obtained from the sale of this pillow lace provided an extremely useful second income, especially when times where hard on the farms and many of the menfolk were getting a pittance for their labour. In 1770, a farm worker earnt seven shillings

Lacemakers in Wootton. One lace making school was situated at Keeley Corner and this picture was taken near to the Church of another school.

and three pence (old money) and by 1892, this had only risen to 12 shillings and six pence. Very young children learnt the craft, often attending lace schools. Well into the 1900's ladies in the village supplemented their family income with sale of this lace. Cecil Caves, born in 1914, whose family lived in Potters Cross, can remember being sent to buy the thread for the lace from Mag Crawley, who lived at the butcher's shop at Keeley Corner (now Pear Tree Cottage). Among other things, she was the agent for Braggins, the Department Store in Bedford. Once the lace was made up, she brought it back from the women lace makers. She herself, a very large lady, always dressed in black, was an expert lace maker. She could be seen in the window of the butcher's shop, with her lace pillow, hard at work. Jean Sherwood, Clerk to Wootton Parish Council, remembers seeing her in the window, when as a child, she visited her grandparents at Keeley Corner. Jean marvelled at how she managed to keep the lace so clean when all around her was evidence of the butchery trade, feathers, innards, blood and gore!! Cecil Caves can remember as a small boy, helping wind the bobbins for his mother. She would work long into the evening, the room lit by an oil lamp with another lamp under her skirts in the winter months, to keep her feet warm. The lace was made to the women's own design but Mag Crawley also sold the linen centres for the women to make into lace doileys.

The Lace Factory

This was housed in what is now two brick built bungalows in the Bedford Road, opposite to Keeley Farm Court. It was built by the owner of Keeley Grange, Sir Arthur Black, M.P., who originally came from Nottingham, the home of machine made lace and was in operation from about 1910 to just after the First World War. The manufacture of this type of lace virtually sounded the death knell for the handmade Bedfordshire variety. The lace factory was in fact a repair shop and girls from other villages as well as Wootton, worked there.

This was the third car to be owned in Wootton. After ten years as a taxi, Mr W. Juffs used it for five years as a bread van and then it became a fish van. When Mr Juff's owned it, petrol was one old shilling and one old penny a gallon (just over five pence).

(LEFT TO RIGHT): *W. H. Juffs (Bill), H. Juffs, Elsie Juffs, Fred Burraway.*

The Bakery in Church Road belonging to the Juffs family. The original cottage was built in 1554, with extensions added over the years. William Henry Juffs bought the building as a smallholding and bakery. On his retirement in 1954, his son William George turned it into a riding stables.

Tennis Racquet Manufacture

One of the more unusual industries in Wootton was that of Henry Trimmings, a member of the Foulks family. From 1933 until 1960, he manufactured and repaired tennis racquets in a small workshop in Cause End Road. At the height of his business, five people were employed. Cecil Caves remembered vividly that Mr. Trimmings could actually play a tune on a strung racquet.

Life in the Early 1920's

Village life was one of self-sufficiency. Almost everything was either brought to the door by travelling shops, grown in the family's allotments or garden or could be purchased in one of the very many shops in one of the "Ends" in Wootton. Cecil Caves' father had three allotments, two in Wootton and one along the Woburn Road, as well as a garden where he kept hens and rabbits. The largest grocery store belonged to Freddy Curtis at Keeley Corner, the double fronted house now number 16. He travelled round the village, from customer to customer, with a selection of goods plus a tank of paraffin for the lamps and heaters. His was not the only grocery establishment. There was one at Tinkers Corner, Patemans, and another in Cause End Road, later to become Caves Store. At one time, it was thought that this site might become the new Doctor's Surgery. When the old house was dismantled, the timbers were incorporated in an extension to a 1480's house in Riseley, the owners of which estimated the Wootton dwelling to be of the Tudor period.

Cecil Caves believes Tinkers Corner was named after a couple of brothers, Joe and Jim Felts who made and mended kettles, pots and pans. There were no less than three bakehouses, Juffs in Church Road, Keeps, where daughter Vera was the pastry cook, in Hall End and one opposite the Memorial Hall run by the Fardell family. Sweets were sold at a shop at the end of Potters Cross, in the Bedford Road, at the bottom of Cause End, kept by Mrs Sid Hutchings (nee Edie Lunnis), at Keeley Corner and at Hall End. Jack Moore, a bricklayer, sold sweets and cigarettes. Connie Robinson remembered another Moore, Fred, who cut most men's hair in the village, in his garden shed in Hall End. Shops were often little more than someone's converted front room. There was also a haberdashers where the Post Office now is and the village cobbler, Stan Faulkner was almost next door, at Swan Cottage. The Post Office itself was in Church Road, again in someone's front room!

The butchers shop was at Keeley Corner, now Pear Tree Cottage, run by "Light" Vincent, brother to Mag Crawley, the lace agent. Renowned for the production of black puddings, it had its own slaughterhouse with its own special smell that both Sid Cook and Cecil Caves remembered vividly! Later on, at least two milk rounds were operating, one run by the Brown family from Keeley Corner and the other by the Sanders family of Bedford Road. Customers would leave their jugs out on their window sills and the fresh milk would be measured into them. Electricity did not arrive in Wootton until the mid 1920's and so tasks like milking were all undertaken by hand. At the Brown's farm, their cows were milked this way until long after the Second World War.

In fact, villagers had little need to travel outside the village at all. The local carriers did go in to Bedford each week and could take passengers. The first bus in Wootton was a single decker coach operated by Jack Dawson, son of the landlord of the Cock Inn. His sister, Jessie, was the conductress. His vehicle was an ex War Department one, dating from the First World War, with solid tyres, a canvas roof and slatted seats. The route to Bedford was from the Chequers, the Church, Cock Inn, Potters Cross, Keeley Corner and then other stops in Kempston. Apparently, the fare was nine old pence (approximately four new pence)!! A treat twice a year, in February and November, would be to visit the Co-op in Bedford on 'Divi' day. Another treat would be to go on the motor train on the Bedford to Bletchley Line. But such travel outside the village was rare as almost every service could be obtained within the Parish boundaries.

"Take aways" are not new to Wootton folk, a fish and chip shop operated before the Second World War on land opposite the Fox and Duck. It closed during the War but re-opened after and finally closed about 1954. It also sold wet fish and was run by Harry Farrar, from Cranfield. The old tin building is now a garage in Potters Cross!!

Children had more freedom, out playing most of the day. A pastime was bird catching. Hedges were taller and overgrown and birds were numerous. When the birds were roosting, one person would be each side of the hedge with a trap. They would make a noise and the birds, frightened, would fly up. Linnets and songbirds might be kept in cages, and sparrows were for pies or fed to the ferrets. Thrushes, brown and green linnets, chaffinches, yellow hammers, robins, wrens, bullfinches and cuckoos, would inadvertently be included. On one occasion, a lad climbed a few trees, bagged 36 rooks and sold them for 1/2p each. Naturally he was in trouble with the gamekeeper as there would be very little sport for visitors.

The first road in Wootton to have tarmacaddam was Bedford Road, then known as the High Street. Sid Cook's father, Charlie, worked for the Council as a roadman. In the summer months, the gangs of roadmen worked with a man driving a steamroller, the men spreading the tar and grit and then the steamroller rolling in the grit the men spread. In the winter months, each roadman was responsible for a length of road. They would edge them, using a piece of string to keep it straight, dig out the gullies, and on frosty mornings, scatter the sand to stop the traffic slipping. Charlie Cook was responsible for Cock Road (now Fields Road) and part of the Woburn Road. He kept his wheelbarrow at CP Cottage and would walk along in the middle of the road, towards Stewartby, spreading the grit. In those days, most of the "traffic" would have been bicycles!

Sport and Leisure

Sport and leisure in Wootton during the 1800's was confined to the wealthier, who had both the money and the time to follow their pursuits. It was only towards the end of the century, in the 1880's, that the "blue collar" workers began to have the time and money to participate in sporting activity. Such sport that did exist was limited to Fetes and Galas organised by the landowners or the clergy.

The Hunt

From 1845 onwards, there were reports of the Oakley Hunt meeting in Wootton, a tradition that continued until after the Second World War. In 1938, the Hunt had a particularly frustrating meet. The headline in the Bedfordshire Times stated, "Plenty of foxes found in Wootton". However, they proved both fit and elusive, taking the Hunt all the way beyond the Three Horseshoes before doubling back and losing the pack. A further "short hunt" from How Wood to Picks Hill also failed despite several sightings of the quarry in a field of kale. Apparently the scent was very poor. This run of bad luck seemed to have resulted in a new strategy as they were reported to have met at 7 a.m. on their next visit in the September but there were no kills reported.

Steeple Chase Match

On 13th January 1848, in the Bedfordshire Times, there was an account of a horse race in Wootton. "On Wednesday last a race came off at Wootton about five miles from Bedford, between Alexander and the Gardener, two steeple chase horses whose comparative merit have, for some time past, been warmly discussed. The match was eventually made up for 150 sovereigns to give the Gardener 10lbs. The course selected for the event was from the large ground in front of Wootton House over the farm of Mr. Hollis, whose homestead was the turning point, and back to the starting field; thus affording about four miles of good hunting country with about a score of fair fences, some posts and rails, and a "yawner" by the little wood.

About four o'clock the horses came up to the starting field, and this was the entry:-

| Mr. Bevill's | Alexander, aged 7 yrs. | 11st. 3lbs. |
| Capt. Armstrong's | The Gardener, 6 yrs. | 10st. 7lbs. |

The account of the running may be summed up in a few words. Alexander made the running at a slow pace, the other horse keeping handy, until they came to the big jump under the wood, which was well cleared by both, without a mistake; here Alexander put on the steam and they both went at a merry pace over the country. The fences were all cleared well – there was no 'interesting incident' to amuse the lookers on – not even a variation in the order of the running, for the Gardener never got in front at all. Alexander pursued the even tenor of his way, and ran in an easy winner. The fact is, he took the lead and kept it, and the Gardener's goose was safely cooked long before it came to anything like racing."

Gaming

In 1846, the Rev. James Jenkyn was reported as having a game licence issued, at a cost of £4 10 shillings, and Peter Pilgrim was appointed by

A familiar site in Church Road were horses from the Riding School. After the bakery closed, Bill Juffs turned the buildings into a very successful and popular riding establishment. He himself favoured the horse and trap as a method of transport and could often be seen out and about the roads of the village.

The Oakley Hunt meeting outside the Chequers Public House in Hall End.

Henry Bolero as Gamekeeper to the Manor of Wootton. Poaching and other offences under the Game laws were serious and stiff punishments could be metered out. On 13th January 1849, Robert Moore was sent to the House of Correction, by the magistrate, Rev. T. B. Whitehouse, for three months. No Game licences were issued that year.

Cricket

1880

The earliest reference to cricket in Wootton was in 1880 when there was a match report of a game against a Kempston side. All games organised during this period were "friendlies". A very close game at this date, against Bromham resulted in a win from the home side. Wootton 77, Bromham 75, a few players were more than a bit hot under the collar after this close finish. Funds needed to be raised to support the team and in 1884 there was a report of a social evening including a string band. Another account of a match against Kempston 2nd XI, in 1890, had Wootton declaring at 156 for 7, a match they were hoping to win. But owing to the dilatory manner in which each man came to the wicket, the game ended in a draw, with Kempston making 21 for the loss of 7 wickets!

1896

In 1896, the Beds and District Cricket League was founded. In 1900, a "revived" Wootton Cricket Club played on Whit Monday in a field lent by Mr. Frossell, a local farmer (Mrs Frossell provided the teas). They beat Biddenham after scoring only 56 with Mepham and Lambert scuttling out Biddenham for 24. This resulted in a second innings by both sides and Wootton managed 58. Biddenham, however, fared even worse with 14. Mepham: 5 overs, no maidens, 10 for 18. Lambert: 4 overs, 3 maidens, 12 for 20! If these bowling figures from the Beds Times are to be believed Biddenham were allowed a third innings!

In 1911 and 1912, the Secretary of the Cricket Club was Mr. W. H. Mepham, School House, Wootton. The treasurer was Mr. G. Line from

Hall End, Captain was Mr. F. Whitbread. In 1911, the Vice Captain was Mr. C. Lowe and in 1912, Mr. F. Loft. The Committee included Messers T. Burraway, H. Line, W. G. Mepham, H. Sinfield, W. Loft and H. Moore.

1920

After the First World War, in 1920, Wootton Hall End picked up the baton and played in the league. Their ground was in the field at the rear of the Chequers, hence their name, where it was stated that special topsoil was shipped in to create, reputedly, the best wicket in the area. During 1920, they managed to finish 3rd in the Beds League Division Two (Southern Section). But in 1929, they won the league.

1930

By 1930, Wootton Hall End had grown and two teams were playing in Division Two and Division Three (Southern Section). A team list for the Second XI includes some very familiar Wootton names:- H. Gilbert, B. Ashpole, E. Burraway, L. Jessup, B. Biggs, A. Biggs, J. Burraway, A. Saunders, W. Caves, V. Ashpole, T. Jiggles, H. Burraway, W. Hutchings and P. Ellis.

1939

In 1939, the year the Second World War broke out, Wootton won the Beds League Division Two (Southern Section). Due to heavy rains and the war, the league fixtures were not all completed, and Wootton were declared the League Champions. Those representing the village at that time were N. Milton, P. Milton, B. Saunders, E. Hutchings, H. Fuller, P. Fuller, F. Loft, S. Loft, L. Keep, F. Jackson and L. Smith.

1964

From that time, right up to 1964, cricket was not played in the village. The pitch in the Chequers meadow was ploughed up during the war. In February 1963, the "County Playing Fields Association" advised the Council that because the work, for which they were prepared to give a Grant, had not been done in the Recreation Field, the Grant would be cancelled. Mr. Jack Hale then lobbied locals, to create an interest and a

Cricket Team taken in 1893 in front of the Old Vicarage in Church Road, since demolished.

Back row (LEFT TO RIGHT): W. Granby, D. Robinson, C. Hodges (gamekeeper), R. Walker, W. Haynes (blacksmith), H. Sinfield, V. R. Bennett (gardener).
Middle row (LEFT TO RIGHT): R. Keep, W. Mepham, F. Buck, C. Sinfield (senior), W. Line.
Front row (LEFT TO RIGHT): T. Burraway, C. Dillon, G. Foster, J. Robinson.

Probably the most successful Wootton Cricket Team, pictured here in 1978.

Back row (LEFT TO RIGHT): Richard Freestone, Roger Loft, Nick Timmins, Simon Fuller, Graham Billing, Nigel Robinson, Arthur Brittain, Christine Ashpole (scorer), Ben Ruffhead, Clifford Fuller.
Front row (LEFT TO RIGHT): Pete Robinson, Ivor Robinson, Martyn Ashpole, Russell Brittain, Steve Clarke, Tony Brittain.

wicket was ready for the 1964 season.

Wootton re-entered the Beds League and were placed in Division Three. They carried on from where they left off in 1939 they won Division Three in their very first season. The victorious team was J. Beard, D. Peters, B. Holmes, M. Freestone, B. Armstrong, M. Jenkins, E. Hall, P. Harris, R. Craddock, P. Orchart and F. Loft. Much of the success was due to the dynamic bowling of Peter Orchart. Wootton made sure of the title against North Crawley, with Orchart's figures of eight wickets from eight balls. One name common to both successful teams before and after the war, was Fred Loft, one of the village lads good at most sports. In the Hospital Cup, they reached the third round and lost to Harpur Sports, who dismissed Wootton for 18 runs.

Wootton Cricket Team 1964.

Back row (LEFT TO RIGHT): Jack Hale, Roger Loft, Dennis Peters, John Beard, Barry Holmes, Mick Freestone, Brian Armstrong, Melvyn Jenkins, Stan Loft.

Front row (LEFT TO RIGHT): Eric Hall, Pete Harris, Fred Loft, Roger Craddock, Peter Orchart.

1965-1978

During this period, the 1st XI maintained a high standard in the Beds Premier League, dropping down to the First Division only three times. The Club managed to run two teams due to the abundance of talent, particularly youngsters. The Second XI won Division Four in 1969 and again in 1976. In 1980, the seconds were in Division One and the 1st XI were top of the Premier Division. Successes were abundant during the 1980's both in the league and Knockout Cup, the Club doing the double three years on the trot. Players representing the Club in the late 70's, early 80's were G. Billing, A. Brittain, S. Fuller, R. Freestone, M. Keens, N. Robinson, P. Robinson, I. Robinson, S. Woolgar, A. Ashpole, M. Burraway, J. Barton, B. Russell, L. Ward, M. Carlton, T. Brightman, G. Robinson, D. Hogg, I. Grummitt, D. Burraway, P. Sanders, N. Timmins, D. Titchmarsh and B. Ruffhead. In 1978, Wootton won the Sharman Shield.

1990-1

Nail biting finishes were the order of the day. When Wootton met Oakley in the Bedford League Cup, everything rested on the last ball of the match. Wootton had scored 160 for 8 off their 36 overs, thanks to "man of the match", Martyn Ashpole, Mick Keens and Pete Robinson. Oakley needed six to win, despite a gallant effort only two were scored, so Wootton won.

Again in 1991, Wootton won the League Cup, beating Thurleigh in a close game by 18 runs. The main run makers were Tim Pendall 68, Pete Robinson 37 and Nigel Robinson 35 (Pete Robinson having scored a century the day before in a league match).

1992

This turned out to be the last season in the Village. The 1st XI finished third in the league.

Soon more football pitches took over on the Recreation field and cricket square, in use for 28 years, disappeared.

Bedford Homing Society

Frequent mention is made in the local press of Wootton families excelling in the Bedford Homing Society. Pigeon racing was popular and in 1938, Will Juffs won a race, which started, from Thurso in Scotland (468 miles from Wootton, averaging as much as 70 miles per hour) whilst Sam Hutchings took his hobby to the Second World War. He spent his time abroad, mostly in India, looking after pigeons for the armed forces. George Loft, Bob Rawlings, Dick Loft and Ron Bellamy featured often in race reports.

Rugby

In 1897 the Beds Times reported briefly that a Wootton XV played against a Marston XV in what appears to have been a rugby game. A goal, a try plus conversion each was the result after 'a most exciting and close game'. However, the sport did not appear again in the village, until the Upper School arrived.

Football

The earliest records of football date back to 1890, when Wootton Blue Cross was formed. In those days home matches were played behind the Cock Inn, where the 'newer' part of Payne Road now is.

The club patron was Sir Philip Payne, whilst other famous locals, Colonel Dillon and Reverend Foster, were also involved in the running of the Club. Opposition teams included such sides as Elstow, Queens Park Excelsior and Kempston. In 1900, Wootton fielded two teams, the Blue Cross and the Rovers; the Blue Cross seemed the senior side, with many references to Rovers players being called up to play for the Blue Cross. Occasionally two matches were played, one after the other with only a break of 15 minutes. Travel to away matches was obviously a different

Wootton Blue Cross Football Team, 1910–11.

Back row (LEFT TO RIGHT): Harry Sinfield, David Robinson, Frank Smith, Bill Mepham, Tom Billing, Barn Walker, Tom Burraway, Fred Milton, Dunny Lovell.

Second row (LEFT TO RIGHT): Billy Gilbert, Monkey Lowe, Stan Faulkner, Jim Walker, Jack Lowe, Jesse Lovell, Arty Robinson.

Front row (LEFT TO RIGHT): Jack Biggs, ?, Russell, Ted Cooper, Lewis Broughton (who came from Bedford).

---

affair to nowadays and early club records show ledger entries for the stabling of a horse! A phantom 'Red Cross Team' was reported as playing, the morning after a particularly successful social evening, where a 'high time had been had by all'!

The Bedford and District League was formed in 1904 and Wootton was amongst its founder members and were rewarded for their efforts by winning the Division Two trophy in 1906-7. The team reflected the prominent families of the village with Burraways, Bensons, Miltons and Lowes amongst its members.

Despite the appalling losses of men folk in the First World War, the inter war years saw the team and its organisation really take off, with first, second and junior sides all competing for local honours. Home matches were played at such varied locations as Fishers Field (where Popes Way now stands), Tinkers Corner (corner of Keeley Lane and Hall End Road) and of course, the present Recreation Ground. Trophies regularly came the way of the Blue Cross, with the Bedfordshire Minor Cup won in 1923 and a succession of Bedfordshire League Championships in the 1930's, thanks to the prolific goalscoring of such players as William Burraway and Frederick Loft.

Two players emerged from the ranks to become football league stars – Arthur (Spratty) Biggs went to Arsenal and Arthur (Harpie) Russell was signed by Bolton Wanderers. In 1938, when Arthur Biggs had just signed for Heart of Midlothian, he returned to Wootton and on Monday January 24th was married. His former friends at the Blue Cross formed a guard of honour with an archway made with some of their old boots!

By this time, the Blue Cross had become the main sporting focus for the village and a couple of untimely deaths were widely reported. Frederick (Sonny) Baker, an 18 year old from Potters Cross, reported to have been an exceptional runner and a promising footballer, had colleagues from the brickyards and the Blue Cross attending his funeral and the death of staunch committee member, William Loft, was also a blow.

The Committee that ran the club was chaired in those days by Mr. Albert Robinson and in 1939; the club was accepted to join the South Midlands League. However, the arrival of hostilities with Germany put paid to any aspirations for six years and the league was suspended and during this time the club competed in local Bedford League tournaments. With so many local men being recruited into the Armed Forces, it was hard to always field a full team. Fishers Field was ploughed up for the war effort.

Reports of matches during the war years were few and far between and the Blue Cross turned to the youth of the village to provide a team. Wootton Juniors flourished with names such as L. Burraway and R. Brightman appearing. The youth were also helping the War effort; the Scouts collected over 14 tons of waste paper. The search for young talent continued and in 1944, the Juniors announced that 18-year-old Aub

Stringer was their new recruit from Lynton Works.

After the war, the South Midlands league seemed to suit the Blue Cross boys and in 1947-8 they were the first ever winners of the Premier Division. The title was decided with a 2-0 victory at Cambridge Town and four coach loads travelled to watch this match. Celebrations went on late into the night.

The United Counties League was joined in 1955 and in their first season the team finished a creditable fourth. But the team's heyday came in the late sixties and early seventies, when, under manager Doug Field, they won the Division Two Cup in 1965, the Division Two title in 1968 and 1970 as well as the valuable Hinchinbrook Cup tournament five times between 1966 and 1971. The Bedfordshire Senior Cup was also lifted in 1971, thanks to a 1-0 victory over Leighton Town on Luton Town's ground. The trophy was presented to club Captain, Phil Burraway, who despite lucrative offers from other clubs, made 1,006 first team appearances – something of a local record.

Wootton's senior status became threatened in the early seventies with the formation of the United Counties League Premier Division. To accommodate matters the club moved to their present home, Weston Park, in 1972 and with the help of many volunteers, a clubhouse and stand were built. Floodlights were added in 1987. These facilities have gradually been expanded to somewhere which can cater for large functions.

The team's best season in the United Counties League Premier Division was runners up in 1980-81 and two years later, they picked up the League Knockout Cup. Most years since have seen mid table security each season, although in 2001, the Bedfordshire Senior Cup was lifted again.

Other men's teams have also been around, particularly since the 1970's, mainly as representatives of local public houses. All of the village's pubs have had football teams, the most successful being from the Fox and Duck, who won the Sunday League Premier Division on three occasions in the 1980's. There are currently teams representing the Black Horse, The Chequers, The White Lion and the Fox and

Duck (known as Wootton Wanderers) and all enjoy various levels of success.

Youth football began in earnest in 1978 when a group of youngsters asked Clifford Russell (son of Arthur Russell of Bolton fame), to manage their under 14 team. Training by the first ever Wootton Rangers was on a Saturday morning and consisted of a kick around while Cliff read the paper! Nowadays there are up to 100 children training on a Saturday morning of varying ages and abilities. The club is run by a solid group of volunteers and many youngsters have gone on to become stars of Wootton Blue Cross, whilst some have gone even further. Chris Willmott was the first ever Woottonian to play in the Premiership, when he made his debut for Wimbledon in 1999.

The Later Years

In recent years there has been a proliferation of sporting choice for the people of Wootton. Indoor sports have become very popular with active teams participating in pool, darts, skittles, dominoes, cribbage and carpet bowls. Other sports such as tennis and table tennis have come and gone whereas the village has a thriving Badminton Club. Some of the pubs have boule courts and one even hosted a cycling group. The building of the Upper School has further enhanced choice and opportunity with several sports not previously available. As well as the more traditional options of football, netball and cricket the curriculum also has included amongst others, rugby, hockey and volleyball. Village based clubs have started as a direct result of the school's initiative and have provided members of a very high standard, capable of competing at county, regional and occasionally international standard. The floodlit all weather complex built by the Parish Council, also provides facilities for 5-a-side football and tennis. All of this activity thrives alongside the long established sports and although there is not currently a cricket team, the Blue Cross especially, maintains its success and has even embraced semi professionalism.

1927 production of Alan-a-Dale performed by members of Wootton Women's Institute in the grounds of the Old Vicarage. Perhaps fortunately for the ladies of the cast, no names survive!

Wootton Womens Institute

The W. I. (Womens Institute) was founded in Canada in 1897. It was encouraged in its activities by the Agricultural Organisation Society and then in 1915, by the Board of Agriculture. Once the idea had spread to England, organisers were sent out into the countryside to encourage institutes to start up in the villages. This was at the time when the woman's place was "in the home", before they had the vote and it was quite a revolutionary idea. The first county to have institutes was Sussex. Bedfordshire's first County Chairman was Miss Foster, daughter of the Vicar of Wootton. Miss Foster became one of the visitors touring the County and helping villages to found an institute. Wootton, naturally, was one of the earliest, founded in August 1919. Dunstable was the first, started in 1917. Miss Foster remained County Secretary until 1940 and even after that, would still visit Institutes. There was no office until after she retired and it was an unpaid position. She just had an honorarium of £23 in 1930, rising to £31 in 1934.

Wootton's Institute met monthly but unlike today, it was an afternoon meeting. The inaugural committee meeting was on Thursday 28th August 1919. The first President was Mrs Squire, with Mrs Frossell as Vice President. Miss Squire was both Secretary and Treasurer. Others present at that meeting were Mrs Walker, Mrs Line, Miss Repp, Mrs W. Benson and Miss Keep. Minute Books show that meetings were similar to today's with a speaker, competitions and nice refreshments. Among the first competitions were three best flowers and three best potatoes and one of the first talks was "a demonstration of re-footing a stocking". Members had to be nominated and seconded before being admitted to membership, and there was great rivalry between the ladies from each group of Roads as to who could provide the best teas. The first meeting was on Wednesday September 17th 1919 when as well as the Officials appointed in August, the following ladies formed the Committee:- Mrs Copperwheat from Keeley, Mrs Hare from Wootton Green, Mrs Howes from Bourne End, Miss Keep and Miss Line from Hall End, Mrs Biggs from Cause End, Miss Lovell from Tags End, Mrs Tufnell from the High Street, Mrs B Walker from Mount Pleasant and Mrs W. Benson from Potters Cross. The lecture at that first meeting was "Travels Through Persia", an illustrated talk with maps, by Capt. G. F. Squire.

By the end of 1919, there were 77 members and by the end of 1920, 109 ladies had joined.

Between the two World Wars, there were many Drama productions and the Institute had a very active choir. Today, the Institute is still well supported but now meets in the evening.

Wootton Group of Scouts, Cubs, Guides and Brownies

The 1st Wootton (61st Beds) Scout Troop was formed in 1910 under the leadership of Miss Stella Dillon, the daughter of Colonel Dillon, then resident at Wootton House. The Scout movement was founded nationally by Robert Baden-Powell in 1908. The meetings were held in the Church

Rooms which were at the side of the old vicarage in Church Road. The first camp was held at Easter 1912, when the Troop trekked to North Crawley.

The Troop was disbanded at the outbreak of the First World War and re-started in either 1918 or 1919, only to close again in the early 1920's when Miss Dillon married Mr. Skinner and moved to Bromham Hall.

Bert Beard, who then lived at Wood End, is believed to have been the first Patrol Leader and other early members were Hugh Denton, Moses

Wootton Scout Troop 1937.

Back row (LEFT TO RIGHT): Ted Stevenson, Norm Russell, J. Gilbert.

Second row (LEFT TO RIGHT): B. Moore, T. Hall, J. Loft, Ken Trimmings, Pete Field, ?, L. Burraway, Ron Brightman, ? Keep, G. Loft.

Third row (LEFT TO RIGHT): Arthur Redman, Ken Granby, Dennis Boyles, Alan Crowsley, Roy Keep, Freddie Burraway, Maurice Boyles, Toffie Poole, Norman Gilbert.

Fourth row (seated) (LEFT TO RIGHT): K. Redman, J. Bull, Rev. Charles Squires, Les Egan, Pym Brew, Arthur Turland.

Front row (on ground) (LEFT TO RIGHT): C. Moore, M. Ellis, Eric Hall, Stanley Poole, D. Jones, Fred Granby.

Rev. Squires was Vicar from 1918 to 1940 and was a great supporter of all activities in the Parish.

Wootton Scout Troop, just after the Second World War.

Back row (LEFT TO RIGHT): Assistant Commissioner, Arthur Sanders, Barry Gilbert, Trevor Moore, John Redman, Cyril Copperwheat, Harold Biggs, Mr Harold Coy (Skip).

Front row (LEFT TO RIGHT): Bob Rawlins, Mick Fuller, Geoffrey Hall, John Hutchings, Keith Hutchings, Ken Hutchings.

Redman, Sid Crowsley, Ted Cooper, Fred Church, Jim Lunnis, Bob Green, Joe Green, 'Stibby' Bennett, Bill Stafferton, Bill Pateman, Bill Benson, 'Tank' Tysoe and Sam Gilbert.

Nothing further is known of the Troop until Harold Coy moved to the village and with Les Egan, re-formed the Wootton Troop in 1936. Harold had moved from Kempston where he had been the 'Skip' of the 101st's. Soon afterwards, the first headquarters was put up, a sectional wooden building, in Church Road opposite to Juff's Riding Stables. The Rev. Squires helped with a loan, and soon an extension was needed too. In 1937, the 1st Wootton Cub Pack was formed under the leadership of 'Pim' Brew, helped by Bill Burraway, a former landlord of the Black Horse. During the Second World War, it closed down and was re-opened at the end of the hostilities, by Mrs Beaumont and Mrs Peggy Boston.

The 1st Wootton Brownies began in September 1964, led by Mrs

Ann Johnson and 2nd Wootton Brownies followed in 1969, run by Mrs Jean Sherwood. In between, the 1st Wootton Guides was started by Mrs Julia Cunliffe in 1966 and in 1971 the 2nd Wootton Guides began, led by Mrs Sheena Thomasson.

The Headquarters moved to the present site in 1969, still in a temporary wooden building and the present brick built building was opened in 1976.

A farmers tea, organised by local farming families, in 1953, held in the Old School.

Bottom row (RIGHT TO LEFT): George Redman, Jesse Lovell, Emma Lovell, Walt Redman, ?.

Second row (RIGHT TO LEFT): Charlie Lowe, Sammy Beale, Polly Lowe, Mrs Campion, Elizabeth Pyner, Will Fuller, Myra Fuller, Kate Thompson, ?, Beat Faulkner, Liz Burraway, Tom Burraway, Stan Faulkner.

Third row (RIGHT TO LEFT): Mrs Benson, Caleb Benson, Charles Fuller, ?, George Russell, Sarah Russell, Alice Carr, Kate Lovell, Jesse Boyles, (rest of row not known).

Fourth row (RIGHT TO LEFT): ?, ?, Freddie Brooks, George Cornish, Mrs Moore, Jack Moore, Mrs Lambert, Mrs Burraway, ?, Lucy Walker, Barn Walker, Jack Robinson, ?, Ginny Redman, ?, Doris Stanton.

Some of the original members of the Evergreens Club.

Left side of table: Cicely Hale, ?, Nellie Gough, Mr Watson, Mrs Watson.
Right side of table: Alice Copperwheat, ?, Freddie Brooks, Sid Lowe, ?, ?, ?, Sara Hills.

Ballooning

Ballooning has always had an element of risk attached to the sport, much more so in the 'old days' as the following three examples illustrate.

1. The Rogue Balloon

A stray balloon caused much speculation in 1891. Two men saw the balloon drifting at low-level near Kempston Hardwick, no sign of any occupants. They managed to catch a trailing rope when the balloon became caught in a hedge at nearby Wootton. The balloon was deflated and the local police took charge of it. Police enquiries failed to solve the mystery, until following a newspaper report, when two London balloonists claimed the remains. They had launched from Battersea, but their flight had gone badly wrong. The balloon had descended near

Neasden and struck the ground, throwing one man out. Thus lightened, the damaged balloon then soared up rapidly, severely frightening the remaining occupant. When the balloon again descended, near Harrow, he jumped out and left the balloon to its fate. In this damaged state it had reached Wootton before finally collapsing.

2. *The Kempston Balloon*

A tragic accident occurred in Kempston, at the flower show held at the Hoo in August 1926 on land owned by Colonel Eugster. The gas balloon 'Miranmar', built and operated by C. G. Spenser & Sons, was one of the attractions at the show, being tethered by a winch to a height of 600ft. After a dozen or so successful ascents, a trailing rope caught in a tree when the balloon was at 100ft. It seems that the ground crew misunderstood the pilot's winching instructions and in the confusion the balloon's netting was ripped away, killing four passengers and the pilot, E. T. Willows. Following the accident Spenser & Sons were fined £100.00 for not having a permit to fly and a further £50 for not having a certificate of airworthiness.

A postscript to this event: Mrs Doyne-Ditmas, daughter of Sir Philip and Lady Payne desperately wanted a ride in the balloon but no one would sell their ticket to her.

3. *Inherent Dangers*

A cross-country flight was one of the tasks that an aspiring aviator had to undertake before obtaining his balloonist's licence. This was the purpose of Henry Cook in May 1906 when he took off from Crystal Palace in London in the balloon 'Vivienne III'. He appeared to be set for a flight to Northampton, but a change in the weather brought about a precautionary landing at Stagsden. The balloon could possibly have flown over Wootton. The sight of the balloon getting closer to landing attracted a crowd of onlookers and disrupted the village cricket match. Cook landed successfully, and with the help of the spectators was soon safely tethered. Unfortunately, the gas valve was found to be leaking. Cook warned about the risk of fire, but before the field could be cleared an explosion took place.

Eight people suffered burns as a result of the explosion, some seriously, and first-aid was given by the village policeman until a doctor arrived.

The pilot's warnings had apparently been ignored, for investigators later found a clay pipe and matches amongst the debris.

Some of the Older Properties in the Village

Keeley Grange

Among the manor houses that were at the centre of each Manor, Keeley Grange still remains. The site is definitely mediaeval and traces remain of the original moat. Still very visible is the pond, on the other side of the road, opposite its main gate, once part of the moat.

The present house was probably built in the mid 1650's; the brick front and porch were added in 1837. The rear of the house still shows the original beams and brick construction

In the 18th century, the manor and house belonged to the Cornish family and by 1790; the owner of the house had become Admiral Robert Gambier, passing on his death, to his son Charles. In 1884 the property was inherited by Miss Polhill and then in 1910, it was sold at auction, to Sir Arthur Black M.P.

Sir Arthur Black owned the "lace factory" opposite, where machine made lace was repaired and also generously donated the land the Memorial Hall stands on. The Hall itself was brought from Ampthill Park after the First World War, where it had been the Sergeants Mess. It was intended as a social and recreational centre for the young men of the village on their return from war service.

In 1926, Keeley Grange was sold to Mr. Higgins and finally belonged to the Wiles family in the early 1950's until 1995.

There has been a suggestion that John Keeley or Kelying, the Chairman of the Quarter Sessions of the Bedfordshire Bench in 1660, once stayed here. His main claim to fame in Bedfordshire was that he sentenced John Bunyan to his first term of imprisonment. However, John Keeling's home was at Southill, and the records at the Bunyan Museum in Bedford show that the three Judges actually stayed at the Swan Inn, Bedford during the trial. Keeley Grange derives its name from the Manor of Keeley or Culy.

157 Bedford Road, a Former Farm House

Once the home of Harry and Ethel Brown who produced and delivered milk and dairy items to the residents of the village. It is situated on the eastern parish boundary with Kempston and is the last house on Bedford Road.

The building is in an "L" shape formation, the rear part is the oldest being 16th century, the front being late 17th century. This is evident by the difference in the beams, the oldest being almost twice the size. The rear part has no formations, the front has a large plate supporting the walls.

There are two inglenooks, one having a large cast iron fireback. One of the three front bedrooms has an open fireplace and the front bedroom walls are wattle and daub. The roof is clay peg tiles.

In 1955 the only facility in the building was a soak-away drain, water was drawn from the well daily and cooking was done on a Valor Oil Stove unless a larger meal was required when a kitchen range in the rear inglenook would be lit. Lighting was by oil lamps and candles and a visit to the toilet meant a trip to a small building at the bottom of the garden containing a large bucket lined with straw, no matter what the weather! There were no toilet rolls only neatly cut newspapers threaded on a piece of string. Water was heated in a copper built into the kitchen, which was

(left)

Evacuees from London during the Second World War, outside 157 Bedford Road, Wootton, then the farm of the Brown family, also suppliers of milk to the village. The black and white house in the photograph below is also 157 Bedford Road with the plaster removed. This is how the house would have looked when first built.

(bottom)

157 Bedford Road as it is today, with the old rendering removed.

lit every day and kept full, providing water for washing up etc. and a bath being a rare event. Personal cleanliness was achieved with a large jug and washbasin on a washstand in every bedroom.

Harry Brown rose very early every day to milk his cows, strain and cool the milk, then Ethel would deliver it in her horse and cart.

This account, provided by Rick Sherwood, paints a picture of life that was very typical throughout Wootton for much of the last two hundred years.

Bourne End Farm

Bourne End Farm is another one of the original manor houses of Wootton. High up on the north west borders of the Parish, with excellent views over to Astwood in Buckinghamshire and beyond, the present house was built in 1937 mainly of red Elizabethan bricks, probably made on site. It is the third known house here and today, the moat around the site of the first manor house is very impressive and has been excavated by the present owner, Mr. William Cook, giving a very good idea of the protection a moat would have offered to the farmstead. Also at this farm, is one of the earliest Dutch Barns in the County, erected in 1870.

Ivy Cottage, Church Road

Bought by the present owners as a 17th century farmhouse, experts since have suggested it is much older, probably 14th century. During renovation, a beamed roof has been uncovered, built in the style of Suffolk craftsmen. The house may well at one time, have been twice as large. There is a central hall with a possible gallery. All these features suggest it was a house of some importance and being so close to the church, could well be the original Wootton Manor House before the present Wootton House was built. The outbuildings are 16th century including cart sheds and an old raised granary building. During the construction work in the gardens, a large amount of stone boulders have been uncovered, possibly the site of the old roadway, going through Wootton, past Popes Way, towards Kempston which could well date from Roman times. The House formed part of the Wootton House Estate, survived the threat of demolition when it became semi derelict and was finally sold in 1949 as a private house.

Gray Lodge, 61 Cause End Road

"Gray Lodge" was built in two stages, the first being around 1760. The house was built end-on to the road, the main entrance being to the side of the building. This siting of houses and cottages end-on to the road was common from the Middle Ages until the late 1600's. Several examples of this architectural feature can be seen in other Cause End Road properties; notably the old timbered manor house and its neighbour opposite the "One Stop Shop". Gray Lodge was rather outmoded being built in this way by the mid 18th century.

Around the 1790's a wing was added to the first building causing the house to become "L" shaped. The front door was then sited in grand Georgian style around the back, facing the area known as "Causeways End" – now St. Mary's Road. This newer part was possibly built by one of William Armstrong's sons, (William lived at Wilstead and died in 1845). Certainly his descendants lived at "Bonnie Cott", as it was called, until 1918 when one Charles Armstrong sold the property to Henry and Mary Gladwin.

The Armstrongs seem to have had rather lofty pretensions when they enlarged their farm cottage (for they farmed the land behind it and where the chapel now stands, down to the border of the old manor lands). The window tax of the 1790's certainly caused them to block up one of the windows in the upper storey of the later wing and it has never been re-opened. The grey bricks with which the house is built and which caused the Gladwins to re-name it as "Gray Lodge" came from an old brick pit in the fields behind the Rose and Crown pub in Keeley Lane. There is little to be seen of it now, save a water-filled hollow.

The Armstrongs pretensions to grandeur increased during the 19th century. One of the family invented a new design of plough which came to be manufactured by John Howard at the Britannia Ironworks in Bedford and became known as the "champion plough of England". (See J. Godbers History of Bedfordshire p.467). Whether the inventor of this plough lived at Gray Lodge is not known for certain. However, by the mid 19th century they had acquired enough money to build the Methodist Chapel on their land next door and had a gravel path laid across the garden so they did not have the indignity of walking out on the road to services. Livery buttons bearing the Armstrong badge of an arm holding a weighted bag have been dug up in the garden, along with a Georgian silver teaspoon.

There is a pump, which still stands beside the stable block at the side of the house and this was working until the late 1950's when the water mains were laid. Despite donating the land to build the chapel, the Armstrongs Christian charity seems not to have extended to other residents of Cause End Road whom they charged 1d each time they needed to draw water, their pump being the only source of fresh water. Until the drainage of adjacent land, when St. Mary's Road was created, there was certainly an underground spring or watercourse, as the lawn at the back of Gray Lodge would have a broad green strip across it even in the driest of summers. Cause End owes its name to Roman Causeway (possibly built to avoid the above mentioned watercourse) which terminates somewhere behind the Methodist Chapel.

In 1949 the Gladwins sold Gray Lodge to a couple named Feigl. He was a chemist and his wife set to with a vengeance to modernise the interior of Gray Lodge, putting in a bathroom among other things. The old sits-bath was still outside when in 1951, Group Captain (Dr.) Bellringer bought the property, which has remained in the family ever since. He was the first RAF dermatologist and was a well-known and much liked figure in the village until his death in 1997. He was a keen gardener and filled the garden with many rare and beautiful plants. He also created a fern garden to remind him and his wife of their native New Zealand. The garden with its large trees is now a haven for many species of birds, insect and other animals including the occasional muntjac deer and fox.

Long before the Bellringers purchased the property, Gray Lodge had the reputation for being haunted! A grey lady is supposedly seen from time to time. Certainly poltergeist activity has occurred; the last manifestation of which happened 30 years ago and was personally witnessed by the writer, who understandably was extremely frightened. Since then, a phantom cat has been seen to disappear into thin air and as recently as August 2001 children's laughter and voices were heard by a visitor, coming from an empty bedroom in the middle of the night. These later manifestations are felt to be benign – the family continues to live quite happily at Gray Lodge.

White Lion

White Lion was originally a Beer House belonging to the Higgins Brewery in Bedford, now part of the Bedford Museum buildings. The present house is turn of the century but in 1850 the Pub was described as having five lower rooms, one let as a shop, six upper rooms, two of which were let, a cellar and behind, an acre of ground. Landlord in 1876 was Abel Low, the village carrier and in 1891 it was James Lunniss, father of Bob who funded the Wootton Charity Christmas lunches for the Retired of the Parish. It is now a Greene King Pub.

Black Horse

Another original Beer House first licensed in 1830 when it became the law. The site of this pub originally was two cottages, one where the public bar and part of the lounge is now and one on the site of the present day car park. In July 1829, Daniel Cook, a carpenter of Wootton bought the lease of one of the cottages from Sir William Long of Kempston House. Sir William had in 1803, become the sole owner of the St. Paul's Brewery in Bedford. James Fowler, owner of the Fowler Brewery of Woburn Sands, took over the lease of the Black Horse in late 1829. The pub did not become part of the Charles

The Black Horse, 7 Potters Cross, taken before the extension was built in 1913. The landlord standing at the gate, is Isaac Tomkins and his wife. The front car park was cultivated as a garden. Originally, when the pub was bought in 1824, there was another cottage where the car park now is. Daniel Cook, the purchaser at that time, was a leading non conformist in Wootton and was one of the founders of the Methodist Church. Meetings were held originally in his cottage.

The Fuller family taken outside the Chequers about 1937. Harry Fuller on the left, holding Michael and his wife Phyllis, holding Anthony (Tony). For many years Harry farmed at Hall End.

Cause End Cottage, the home of Mrs Doyne-Ditmas when she returned to the village, after the death of her husband.

The view along Potters Cross, looking back towards the village. Flooding has always been a problem in this road, being the lowest point in the village. The photo dates from just before the Second World War.

Cottages at Keeley Corner, to the right of the Rose and Crown in Keeley Lane.

Cottages along the Bedford Road (the middle ones now demolished and replaced by Walnut Cottage). Once the home of the Sanders family, suppliers of milk to the village.

Wells chain until 1878. The tenants from 1829 onwards were the Cook family. Martha Low daughter of Abel from the White Lion married Caleb Cook from the Black Horse. The Pub became a Free House in 1993.

Rose and Crown

Known locally as "the Legstraps" due to the Victorian fashion for farm workers to tie string around the bottoms of their trousers to stop rats getting up their legs at harvest time. An old property, first licensed as a Public House in the early 1800's it belonged to the John Morris brewery of Ampthill and is now a Whitbread Pub.

Chequers

Again a very old property and the first "Free" House in the village being originally part of the Wootton House Estate. In 1876 it belonged to Miss Smart, a relative of Lucy Monoux, of Eversholt and by 1885, belonged to Sir Philip Payne. Tenants through most of the 1800's were the Line family and they were also farmers. It is now a Charles Wells Pub.

Star Inn

Licensed first in 1847, the Star belonged to the brewery Newland and Nash of Lurke Street, Bedford. It closed in the early 1950's and is now called Astra House.

The Cock Inn

The oldest documented Public House in the village. Bought in 1785 for £125 when the site just had cottages and a blacksmiths on it, by the brewers, Whittingstall and Long of Bedford. The present building is late Victorian and it is now also a Charles Wells pub.

Fox and Duck

Built in 1836 on a field previously belonging to the Cock Inn. Charles Higgins was the first owner and the pub is now part of the Greene King chain. The first tenant, John North, sold his lease back to the Higgins brewery in 1862.

Public Houses were a very important part of village life. Almost all landlords had to have a daytime job, to make ends meet. Checks through the Census returns of the 1800's show such occupations as carrier, shoe repairer, farmer. Charlie Cook, landlord of the White Lion from 1906 until 1924, drove a lorry for the local council and also ran a wagonette, used for day trips to Woburn, as a sideline. Landlords ran sick clubs for their regulars, everyone paying in each week so that should illness occur, families could then get some help when there was little money coming in.

Defence of the Realm

The Early Days

Today we regularly see British troops on the TV news, often as part of the United Nations peacekeeping forces. The concept of a full-time regular army is, however, fairly recent in British history.

Once the Roman legions left, there were no permanent military forces, and armies were raised whenever the need arose. The King would expect each of his lords to provide armed men for military service, and each lord, in turn, would order his tenants to provide their quota of men-at-arms.

Military campaigns were usually short and seasonal, for the men sent off to battle with the army were the same men required to gather in the harvest and all the other essential tasks.

By Tudor times, the rather haphazard feudal system had become better regulated. Each country had a quota of men to be supplied in times of national emergency, into a force that became known as the Militia. The county Sheriff was responsible for keeping records of those eligible for military service.

Following the break between Henry VIII and the Catholic Church, an invasion was expected from France and Spain. At that time Wootton had the requirement to provide two archers and 33 billmen (bill – pike with hook on the end) towards the county quota.

A century later the ravages of the civil war between King and

115

Parliament reinforced the public suspicion of standing armies; after the restoration of Charles II in 1660 the first regular army in Britain was a mere four regiments. The counties were, however, still required to maintain their Militia lists.

The gentry of the county raised a mounted force, which included Sir William Thompson of Wootton, mounted and armed at their own expense. The various parishes were responsible for providing foot soldiers, and five Wootton men listed as part of the Colonel's Company. This was a period of some civil unrest, and the Militiamen received payment of one shilling a day when called to duty.

By 1757, Britain was at war with France. The regular army had grown in size, and was engaged in America and Canada as well as Europe. The Militia force was again raised, for home service only. Within Bedfordshire, eligible men between 18 and 50 years of age were balloted to provide the 400 needed for the country quota. Militia service was for three years, although those selected had the option of providing a substitute if they could do so. In practice, this meant that the wealthier men would pay someone else to take their place.

The ballot was unpopular, as many feared they would be sent overseas, despite the 'home service only' promise. The ballot provoked a riot in Wootton, 'which mutinied, took the list from the Constable and tore it.'

Parish relief was provided for the families of the men that were called up.

By the end of the war in 1763, there were eleven Wootton men in service. As two had enrolled for a second term, they were probably paid substitutes.

The Militia was again embodied during the American Revolution; the Bedfordshire regiment performed garrison duties in Hampshire, Devon, Kent and Essex before being stood down in 1783. One Wootton man certainly paid for a substitute, as William Goddard took the place of Benji Hill, Goddard's family receiving parish support. At this time the Light Infantry Company was commanded by Captain Monoux.

When the threat of French invasion occurred in the aftermath of the French revolution, the Militia was not considered to be an adequate reserve force, and many voluntary groups were formed for local defence.

Bedfordshire alone formed 22 companies of Infantry Volunteers and four troops of Yeomanry Cavalry, possibly one of the benefits being that enrolment as a volunteer gained an exemption from the Militia ballot. Volunteer service was a part-time activity; the Militia still served for three years, and the Bedfordshire Regiment performed garrison duties at Bristol and Exeter.

The French threat ended with the Battle of Waterloo, by which time the Militia were at Norman Cross, near Peterborough, guarding French prisoners of war.

With the dictator Bonaparte in exile, peace was restored. The Militia and Volunteers were disbanded, with the yeomanry following a few years later.

When agricultural unrest broke out special constables were enrolled to deal with the troubles rather than recall the Militia. Disturbances occurred in Wootton and Kempston in 1828 and Wootton Pillinge suffered arson attacks in 1830.

Taken at the time of the First World War. On the left, Percy Sanders, middle, Geoff Mepham, son of the Wootton Schoolmaster, and on the right, Albie Gilbert. Percy went on to be an apprentice car mechanic and Albie lived all his life in Wootton, working at Meltis. He was a member of the Wootton Parish Council for many years and an authority on the history of the village.

The county police were formed in 1840, thus removing the need for the Militia to deal with civil matters. The Militia then took on more of the characteristics of a regular army unit; in 1852 the title of 'Light Infantry' was adopted and in this form the Militia survived, now as volunteers, until army reforms in 1881. From this time the Militia became linked to the regulars as the 3rd Battalion, Bedfordshire Regiment.

World War II

Wootton War Memorial is a testament of the brave men from the village who fought and died for their country, it also makes chilling reading (see Appendix 12).

The memorial originally stood at the bottom of Church Road, in proximity of where the "keep left" island now stands. It was moved to its current position, on land owned by Mr. William Henry Juffs, in October 1966.

In WWI husbands and sons from the same families died, thus depleting what was already a small community. In WWII villagers in the military were more widely dispersed, avoiding a repeat WWI.

After WWI the Memorial Hall, Nissan hut (Sgts. Mess) from Ampthill Park, was purchased with public subscription, instigated by Reverend Squires and Sir Arthur Black, the land being donated by the latter.

Medals

At least two Wootton men received the Military Medal, both of whom served in WWI and survived the conflict.

G. S. Faulkner, a Corporal in the 10th Rifle Brigade. Three months after joining-up he proceeded to the Western Front, where he did excellent work as a Lewis gunner in various sectors. He fought in engagements on the Somme and at Ypres, and was severely wounded at Paschendale in September 1917, which resulted in the loss of a leg. In August 1917

The Wootton War Memorial, in its original site at the end of Church Road. The old School can be seen in the background, built in 1922 on land given by Sir Philip Payne.

(left) Private 3974 Herbert Moore, 5th. Battalion, Bedfordshire Regiment. He died in Malta on Friday 24th September 1915, aged 22 years. He had enlisted in Bedford and his parents, Alfred and Anne Moore, lived in Hall End.

(right) Sergeant Thomas Billing, 3684, 5th Battalion, Bedfordshire Regiment. When war was declared in August 1914, he volunteered and after serving at Bury St. Edmunds, was sent to Gallipoli in the following year. He took a conspicuous part in various engagements on the Peninsular, and whilst engaged in heavy fighting at Sulva Bay, was killed on 15th August 1915. He is commemorated on the Helles Memorial, Turkey.

Corporal Faulkner was awarded the Military medal for conspicuous gallantry and initiative under heavy fire. On his discharge from hospital Corporal Faulkner was demobilised in February 1919.

Corporal Faulkner lived in the High Street, Wootton.

H. Short, Company Sergeant Major, East Yorkshire Regiment, was already serving in 1914. He proceeded to France immediately on the outbreak of war and served during the retreat from Mons. He also fought with distinction in the battles of the Marne, Neuve Chapelle, Festubert and the Somme. Company Sergeant Major Short was awarded the Military Medal for conspicuous bravery and devotion to duty in January 1916. Later in the year he was discharged as time-expired but in October 1916 was called-up again and rendered valuable service as a musketry instructor in Yorkshire until demobilised in March 1919.

Soldiers of the 1/5th Beds. were posted to Palestine, the Dardanelles and Egypt. Four who died in the Dardanelles were:-

Sgt Tom Billing

Tom Billing was a member of the 1/5th Beds, a goalkeeper for Wootton Blue Cross team and also a member of Wootton Cricket Club and played in league matches. He was a jovial fellow, greatly liked and respected by all his comrades.

Lance Corporal Fred Foulkes

Fred Foulkes was a member of the 1/5th Beds and played forward for the Blue Cross team. He was of a retiring disposition, a favourite among his fellow members.

Lt I. T. L. Foster

Lt Foster was the fourth son of Rev. Foster and he was killed in the Dardanelles aged 30 years of age. Lt. Foster was a prime mover in starting the Bedford Volunteer Training corps with 17 friends and eventually the corps numbered nearly 400.

He was appointed Temporary 2nd Lt. in 16th. Durhams. As he had received training in the Officers Training Corps, he was soon promoted

Mr W. H. Juffs and Mrs Annie Juffs. Mr Juffs, the baker from Church Road, is in the uniform of the Bedfordshire Regiment. He was just one of the very many men who served during the First World War and one of the fortunate ones to return.

and selected to go to the Dardanelles, where he was attached to 5th Manchesters. Lt Foster had a brother in Flanders with the Bedfordshire Yeomanry.

Sgt Thomas Richard Butler

Sgt Butler died of his wounds at the age of 25. Thomas was born in Kempston, enlisted in Bedford. He became a resident of Wootton, and both he and his wife lived in Potters Cross.

Memories of WWII

On the eve of the outbreak of WWII, the young people of the village were enjoying themselves at the annual fair held in the paddock behind the Cock Inn.

During the "phoney war" no shortages were evident, although the blackout was in use and preparations were in hand.

At this time the London Brick Company was working on experimental bomb shelters in Field 99, between Stewartby and Marston Moretaine. These shelters would be built up and blown down.

Villagers did secret work in the Coronation Works by Chimney Corner, filling bombs and shells with explosives and manufacturing smoke blocks to be burnt for camouflage. A yellow hue hung around the area.

Early in 1941 Twin Woods and Thurleigh land was surveyed for aerodromes for American forces.

Special Constables and ARP Wardens came into being, assisted by Fire Watchers.

The Home Guard

After Dunkirk the Local Defence Volunteer Unit, Wootton Branch was formed.

Eventually the LDVU became the Home Guard. Initially and contrary to "Dad's Army" image, the Home Guard consisted of young men aged 19 to 25. When call-up age was reduced and young men aged about 20-22 years of age joined the forces, older people joined the Home Guard.

There were two Home Guard posts: one at Bourne End and the other at Wootton Wood, both posts being sandbagged. Two men guarded each post, one hour before sunset and one hour after sunset as these appeared to be the prime times of any bombing raids.

To begin with the American Ross rifles from WWI were used, plus tin helmets and gas masks. As war progressed the weapon used extensively was the Lee Enfield.303 rifle, (also a survivor from WWI). At the time

Wootton and District Home Guard. This photo was taken on the present Recreation Ground near to their Head Quarters, a wooden building which stood where the changing rooms now stand.

Back row (LEFT TO RIGHT): ?, *Charlie Granby, Geoff Smith, Fred Burraway, Les Lowe, Tom Barclay, Reg Hardy, Bob Lowe, Bill Readhead, Frank Waby.*

Third row (LEFT TO RIGHT): Ken Granby, Harry Fuller, Ron Brightman, ?, Mr Weston, ?, Rex Stanton, Mr Holton, Ron Stringer, Jim Whitbread, Fred Haynes.

Second row (LEFT TO RIGHT): Andy Wear, Charlie Burraway, Joe Pedder, Jim Church, Alfie Moore, Mr Crowsley, Len Waby, Jimmy Haynes, ?, Don Haddow, Gordon Keep, ?.

Seated (LEFT TO RIGHT): Bill Parks, ?, Mr Haddow, Joe Sharpe, Ken Attrill, Mr Beard, Harry Shaw, Mr Manyweathers, Geoffrey Frossell, Doug Brightman, Bill Burraway, Rob Redman.

Front row (LEFT TO RIGHT): Harry Tysoe, Ted Rawlins, Don Haddow, Jack Loft, Bob Lunnis.

this equipment was nearly as good as the regular forces.

The firing range was in Stewartby brick pit, now Stewartby Lake. This was also a good area for the practice of throwing hand grenades.

Two men in charge were Mr. Short (Lt) and Mr. Smith (Sgt). Mr. Davies, M.D. of London Brickyard was the chief officer for a time. At one time thirty people had joined; this membership included: Hugh Copperwheat, Vic Caves, Denis Billing, Ray and Roger Beard, Thomas Stevenson, Stan, Fred and George Loft, the Fields family, Ron Rawlins, William Cook, Mr. Saunders, Mick Hawkins, Bob Lunnis, Mr. Redhead, William Cook and Len Smith (son of Sgt Smith), Mr. Fuller, the Lowe brothers, Nobby, Bert (Chummy) and Stan, Lewis, Robert and Archie Redman. They met regularly for drill and field craft.

Out of the Home Guard a little group was formed, Lt. Hockliffe's Commandos. Incidentally Mr. Hockliffe was of the family who owned Hockliffe's Book Shop in Bedford where the Yorkshire Bank now stands. This group spent weekends testing local defences, breaking into aerodromes and general sabotage – their HQ was the Blue Cross. One November morning they had to break into Bedford defences by wading in the river and became extremely cold.

Denis Billing was captured in one set of manoeuvres taking place in Stagsden. He was ordered to get in touch with part of his unit at Keeley Corner and was spied en route.

Occasionally scuffles would break out between the Canadians, billeted in one of the fields in Hall End Road, and the Home Guard.

Three incidents which do conjure up images from the TV series of "Dad's Army" are:

The Home Guard used the Memorial Hall as a makeshift rifle range. One evening believing they had placed enough protection around the interior of the building to prevent .22 bullets penetrating the wall they began shooting. Ray Beard, walking along the road, noticed a shower of bullets leaving the Hall and entering the road! The patch on the end is still there today.

Nobby Lowe related how, on one training exercise, he was instructed to defend a platelayer's hut alongside the railway line near Stewartby.

Realising that if he stayed within the hut, he would be a sitting target, Nobby undertook a more active defence. Climbing a nearby tree, he hurled bricks on the 'attacking' Canadian Infantry, later claiming the bricks simulated grenades. Severe bruising to backs and pride was caused to the Canadians.

On one occasion when there was an exercise between Wootton and Kempston, a cowman, working on a local farm, was excused manoeuvres as he had cows to milk. The cows just happened to be in a field in Kempston so the cowman was able to report on the 'enemy's' position.

Denis Billing, who eventually joined the 159 Infantry Brigade, remembers standing guard over the food storage centre at Chimney Corner.

Naturally, most meetings ended with pints of beer in the Cock Inn.

Evacuees

One Saturday night following the outbreak of war evacuees arrived in Wootton, only they were not supposed to be here – they should have gone to Clapham. These were mums and babies instead of the expected children. They stayed. Mr. Tufnell, Clerk to the Parish Council, and other councillors went around the village encouraging the villagers to take them in. Mr and Mrs. Tufnell took in a mother and two children, but only for a week. Then the evacuees went on to Devon to stay with friends. Other evacuees then stayed with them. Children from the Willesden area of London stayed in a house in Keeley Lane and in one of the bungalows converted from the lace factory in Bedford Road.

The majority of the evacuees thought they had come to the "back of beyond", a totally different experience from London. No street lamps and only outside privvies, certainly no facilities for the influx of mums and babies. For some it was too much and they returned to London the next day, getting a lift to the railway station with Mr Boyles in the coal lorry.

Mr Tufnell soon told them that Wootton did actually receive a daily newspaper and that the villagers were not ignorant. Friendships blossomed between the evacuees and the villagers, many keeping in touch long after the war was over.

The evacuees returned home when the doodlebugs flew over in 1943-44. By this time they had become so used to the countryside that they did not wish to return to London.

School half term was begun for potato picking. Children often spent half days in school if there was insufficient room for all. Half days for local children and half days for the evacuees.

Airmen from Cranfield were the next group to be billeted in Wootton and Wootton Road (Kempston Rural) around the Iron Gate Corner area.

Mr Tufnell kept a pig, and anyone doing so had to give up their bacon ration. Similarly with hens, the egg ration had to go. Families gleaned in the cornfields to feed their hens. Coming to grips with rationing could be very difficult.

The Land Army

Young women were not immune to the call-up; they either joined the forces or went into the Land Army. Mrs McKeegan (Cicely Redman) has mixed feelings of time in the Land Army. She writes:

"At the beginning of WWII, when so many of the young men were called-up including those from farms, etc. girls were asked to volunteer to work on the land, taking on jobs in the dairy, fields, forestry and market gardens. Thousands of girls then joined the Land Army during the next few years. I was one of them – life was very different from the sheltered upbringing I had up to then but although sometimes it was very hard it was also worthwhile.

Living in a hostel with 19 other girls was the first hurdle – me being an only child. Getting up very early each day to race for the bathroom and then pack sandwiches for the day (first come had the choice!). After breakfast we went off in groups by truck to the farms or fields as required.

I started in a field hoeing cabbages and other vegetables – rows and rows of them! Sometimes we set potatoes by hand – field after field. (Oh!

Our poor aching backs). Later in the season we had to pick them up again. There was lettuce and beetroot to single out, in fact any vegetable garden job that needed doing.

We worked in all weathers – getting sunburnt in summer making it difficult to lay down at nights – to trying to pick Brussels or cut cabbage covered in frost and ice with mittens that were useless once wet, hands so cold making it very hard to hold a knife!

Later on I went to farms and helped with the corn – firstly we had to gather the sheaves and stand them in "stooks" to allow them to dry before being carted to the threshing machine. Heavy work throwing the sheaves up onto the machine, even more dicey to be standing on the top cutting the strings off the sheaves before dropping them into the drum – especially when they contained a nest of mice! We tied string around our trouser legs in case they looked for a quick escape route!

Some of us had jobs on dairy farms feeding and tending the cows, cleaning out the sheds, etc., feeding the calves was a lovely job, (I'd never heard of veal then).

Being on a milk round meant that I had to learn to drive – I had a one-hour lesson, not knowing even where reverse was, before driving the van out on the round! Carrying a two gallon can of milk from door to door, pouring it from a half-pint measure into a jug provided by the householder. How different from today. Of course the milk first had to be poured from 10 gallon churns on the van to the two gallon one. (Good for the muscles).

I also did quite a bit of tractor driving, including fetching a new Fordson Major from the Ford Garage in St. Peters, Bedford and driving to Box End, (this was the latest model then).

On another farm I did poultry plucking and dressing, delivered 60+ gallons of milk daily to the depot in Bedford, and also helped the farmer with his bookkeeping. Quite a variety wasn't it? No time to get bored.

At that time I was "living out" as they called it. I was lucky and allowed to live at home. The war was over by then and we were waiting to be "demobbed".

Hostel life helped me to mix with all sorts of girls, some were fairly local and some from the other end of the country. We did have some hard times, but there were good times too when, although tired, we all met socially at parties held at the Hostel and were invited to parties elsewhere. We had Supervisors who watched us at these occasions in case anyone misbehaved! If we went out in the evening alone we had to be in by 10pm. Or if a "late pass" was issued, by 12 midnight. (Not many girls were allowed these).

Summer nights meant working late, especially at hay time and harvest, we really could appreciate Harvest Festival when 'all is safely gathered in'."

Cicely's mother had two Land Army girls billeted with her, plus her daughter.

Life on the Farm

The memories of a farmer's son, Frank Cook are best summed up in his own words:

"3rd September 1939: First memory. War being declared and listening to Mr Chamberlain, our Prime Minister, while sitting on the kitchen steps at Bourne End Farm, Wootton.

Next memory. Father and Mother went to Bedford some Saturdays to shop and see the animals sold in the market and to buy and sell corn and feed for our cattle.

On the last Saturday in September we arrived home to find a lady waiting for us with four young boys sent to the country from London because it was expected that Germany would bomb London, the lady said that the boys were to live with us. On looking back it must have been dreadful for them. Two Welsh Cockney boys aged 11 and 13 named, I think, Allan and David Hughes and two boys aged seven and 10 from Neasden, named Bobby and Dennis Kent (?) Their mother had recently died and their father came next day to see them and bring them more clothes and toys.

My poor mother was distraught as to how to cope with four extra boys, so she asked me to show them around the farm while she made tea for us all. The boys, it seemed, had never been on a farm and the first thing the Welsh boys asked me was "Where was the nearest pub and fish and chip shop?" They only stayed one week then went back to London.

Wootton Schools had mainly children from Neasden and Willesden and most of them returned quite quickly. However, some stayed including Bobby and Dennis who moved into the village to be nearer the school. In 1940 many more came and stayed as the Germans had started bombing London very heavily. Wootton then had to find room for all these extra children and their teachers. I think at one time there were approximately six hundred of us all together. Some were taught in the Scouts' Hut, some in the Memorial Hall and some in both chapels. My teacher was a Mr Edwards, a Welsh Londoner, and he was supposed to teach between 50 and 60 of we boys, what a hope, in the Wesleyan Chapel. Lots of games and playtime but not much teaching.

I stayed at home a lot in busy times on the farm. When biking to school I passed a search light based on the hill between Hall End and Wood End and we used to watch its powerful beam piercing the sky at night when enemy planes were about, (not too often). Some of the soldiers working the light used to come and help us in the hay time and harvest. About this time Father was allowed to buy a new tractor (they were rationed). A Standard Fordson costing £110.00. He had an Allis Chalmer Model WC bought in 1938 when we moved from Middle Farm, Cople to Bourne End.

Almost every commodity was rationed and I remember buying the last tin of cough sweets from the shop opposite the school, as there were no sweets at all at that time in the war. They were called Zubes and had "Go suck a Zube" on the tin. Needless to say I had to share them with my mates.

In 1943 we had a pigeon unit from the RAF based on our farm. At that time pigeons were used for sending messages both from planes, the army and from men fighting behind the enemy lines. Anywhere where they did not have a wireless or could not use one. Germany bombed Coventry about this time and the whole sky was lit up with flames, (this is when the Cathedral was destroyed).

At this time we had Land Girls working for us and the first one was Mary Day who had previously worked at Wootton House as a maid to Colonel Grenville and family. In busy times we also had Land Girls brought by lorry from Milton Ernest five days a week. I was not very old but I remember feeling sorry for them as many of them had come from places like Sheffield and from very poor families. They told us they had not owned a pair of shoes when children, but they were nearly always cheerful and often sang as they worked. Later in the war they used to come to work talking about the dances they were invited to at the American Base at Chicksands. The American Air Force personnel were given more pay than our men and gave the girls gifts like silk stocking, etc. not obtainable here.

Once we had a gang of about 20 men from the Free Polish Air Force to help us dig the potato crop and I was fascinated to see that many of them had golden false teeth. They said that it was the custom in Poland and also served as an emergency supply of money.

Air Force and Army and Navy Weeks were sometimes held in the village. Concerts were held in the old school to raise money to send parcels, etc. to the forces abroad. I remember drawing a Spitfire and a bomber for an art exhibition held in the Scouts' Hut and with the help of another boy hoping to make a mile of pennies, only it ended after a few yards outside the school wall. In the concerts anyone who had a talent for singing, etc. took part.

There were no school dinners so my Mother arranged with Mrs Odell (Dorothy Orchart's mother) for me to have dinners with them and their evacuee. Later on I went to Mrs Fardells in Bedford Road.

1944 the Home Guard was issued with some rifles and Bren guns and they had manoeuvres at our farm, which had supposedly been captured by Kempston Home Guard as the enemy. Our cowman, in Wootton H.G., cycled through them and told Wootton of the 'enemy' positions. All great fun for us boys watching and after they had gone we collected a lot of strings of crackers which they used instead of live bullets.

During the war all the gardens and allotments were used for growing vegetables and most householders managed to produce a lot of their needs and some gave to those who could not. Gardeners helped each other by giving away seeds and cuttings, etc. and the school had a plot just outside the school wall where gardening was taught one afternoon a week.

The school was very limited in what it could teach; no woodwork, cookery, science or swimming. Even paints were in short supply and the bus that used to take children to Stewartby before the war was stopped and the swimming pool closed.

On the farm Father had to plough up most of the grass so the ploughed acres rose from 60 in 1939 to 250 by 1945 and so with all these acres in corn we were threshing with a large machine that knocked the wheat out of the ears, just as a combine harvester does today. First the wheat was cut by binder which and bound the wheat in bundles. Then they had to be picked up by hand and stood together, ears on the top so that the seed would dry in the wind. They were then loaded onto carts and pulled by horses and sometimes a tractor and trailer, usually made from an old car chassis. These loads were then taken to the farm buildings and built into stacks large enough to be threshed out in one day later with the machine. If we did not want the corn at harvest time we had to thatch the stacks, with straw, with straw like a house.

The corn came out of the machine and was put into large bags hired from the corn merchants or the railway company. These held 75 kilo of beans and peas and they had to be carried on one shoulder or laying up one's back. The rest of the sheaves, i.e. the chaff and straw were all kept for the cattle to eat or lay on in the cow yards.

I started ploughing with a Fordson Standard, which had steel wheels on it on my 13th birthday, my brother William having taught me how, when I used to take his tea to him down on the field. I felt very grown up, but I must of worried my Mother a lot. I wonder what the safety people would think today.

Mr. Bill Juffs' father was the Wootton baker and delivered twice a week. Mother used to soak the stale loaves in milk and heat them in the oven and they were as good as new. Mrs Juffs was very kind to we boys and used to open a hatch in the bake house wall and give us a new bread roll each to eat as we cycled home from school. Sometimes we would meet army lorries and Bren gun carriers coming from the searchlight camp and we had to jump off the road and drag our bikes up the grass bank because the road is very narrow on that hill.

1945 there were now many thousands of Italian prisoners of war in this country, captured in the North Africa campaign. On the farm we had four every day all year and in harvest we sometimes had six. The Italians were a happy lot and most of them were just glad to be out of the fighting. The discipline in their camp was enforced by the threat of cutting off their hair. They were very proud of their locks and were always combing their hair. Once, one of them, named Victorio, had not returned to the camp by curfew time and the Commander had ordered his hair to be cut off. He came to work in a foul temper and father sent him to work on his own, trimming a hedge. We had never seen a hedge trimmed so quickly before!

One of my worst memories of helpers on the farm was when the authorities started holiday camps for Londoners, one was at Ampthill. They were cockney women of all ages. We had them to help hoe the large acreage of root crops grown for the cattle. Just imagine a 16-year-old lad in charge of 20 of them. I did not know when they were teasing and could not understand what they were saying when talking in cockney slang, e.g. having a cup of 'Rosy Lee' and far more unintelligible sentences but as we had to pay them I was expected to get them to hoe the crop, (I guess I learnt quite a lot). I certainly had a laugh when after taking most of their clothes off the first day to get brown, they came to work on the second day wearing pyjamas as they were so sunburnt not having seen much sunlight before.

After these, we were sent German prisoners. They were not so happy, but very sad. The older ones did not want the war and the young ones had been brainwashed by Hitler's gang. As I worked alongside them and talked to them, few of them would find fault with Hitler. The ones we did not like were from Eastern Germany, mainly officers, and they believed they were the superior race and hated doing manual work. When the war ended we had become friends to some and when they went home Mother gave them a food and clothing parcel as their letters from home showed how bad conditions were in Germany.

132

Some other memories: I used to watch the American Flying Fortress planes leaving and some of them returning, although a lot were shot down when they went on daylight raids over Germany. We could see Thurleigh Aerodrome quite clearly from Bourne End Farm. I remember seeing a German bomber in daylight over Stewartby. I also remember being fitted with a gas mask and having to carry it on my bike to school and being told off by the teacher when I forgot it.

I kept maps of the war's progress from Africa to Berlin and could recognise all English 'planes and many German ones – I enjoyed drawing them.

Late one evening, soon after D-Day when the allied armies invaded Europe, the sky was filled with our bombers, Lancasters and Stirlings, all pulling gliders full of troops. They flew over us for nearly an hour. The troops were sent to capture the bridge at Arnhem in Holland to stop the Germans blowing it up and to create a diversion behind their main defence line. I shall never forget those hundreds of 'planes and gliders droning over us. Sadly, many of the men were killed, mainly due to them being dropped on the wrong side of the river and too far apart. Also, unknown to the allies, the Germans had kept a division of armoured Panzer troops back near to Arnhem.

8th May 1945 – VE Day. Victory in Europe. I remember biking to Wootton with the Land Girls in the evening. There was a fair behind the Cock Inn and some singing, but people did not seem to know what to do except feel happy that the war had ended at last. However, the forces were still on the battle fronts and did not come home for a long time."

Wings-for-Victory Week
(an extract from the Bedfordshire Times – date unknown)

"Wings-for-Victory Week was declared open on Saturday in the Stewart Recreation Ground by Wing-Commander Hughes, O.B.E., A.F.M. He was introduced by Mr J. Young (Chairman of the Parish Council), and with him on the platform were Mr Tarling (Chairman of the Committee),

Mrs H. Robinson (Secretary) and Mrs Young.

Mr Young, in introducing the speaker, stated that the target figure was much too low and should have been set at £2,000, a figure, which he confidently expected to see, raised.

Wing-Commander Hughes pointed out that small communities such as Wootton, could not raise sufficient money for a bomber or a fighter plane, but their contribution would provide numbers of tools kits for the maintenance of service aircraft and other useful tools for the ground staff of an aerodrome.

The focal point of the campaign was practically centred in or near the Recreation Ground, school and Boy Scout Hut. The Home Guard, under

The new standard for Wootton British Legion was dedicated on 2nd September 1962. The parade marched from the Memorial Hall to the Recreation ground. Holding the furled banner is Mr Harold Coy (2nd from right). 5th from left, front row, Mr Archie Clarke, 6th from left, front row, Mr Reg Ashpole. Mr Len Odell and Mr Ern Wildman are 2nd and 3rd from right, in the far row, nearest the houses.

Lt H. Short had erected and manned numerous sideshows, which, on Saturday, attracted considerable attention. There was also a bring-and-buy stall and a refreshment stall arranged by women's organisations – these did good business and altogether £65.00 was raised.

A fancy-dress competition attracted a large number of competitors. Races for children were arranged by a Committee and in the veterans' race Arthur Beard again "showed his heels" to the rest. In the evening the Royal Engineers arranged a dance in the school.

On Sunday afternoon a Church Parade was held in connection with the Wings-for Victory Week. The parade, which fell-in on Keeley Corner and marched to the Recreation Ground, was disappointed because the band did not arrive. The parade comprised of the Cadet Corps under Sgt Major Smith, Boy Scouts, Youth Club, W.V.S fire guard, N.F.S., Air-Raid Wardens, First-Aid Party, Special Police, and the Home Guard under Lt H. Short and the A.T.S. and R.E. contingents – in fact all organised war efforts were represented.

The assembly was addressed by the Rev. Paradine Frost, the Vicar, and the Rev. T. Quigley opened the service with prayers. Warden F. Tuffnell read the Psalm. The singing was led by the Wootton and District Choral Society.

The collection, taken on behalf of the RAF Benevolent Fund, amounted to over £24.00."

War in General

After Dunkirk 'things' tightened up and all public building came to a halt. Blast walls were built in Stewartby village and rationing began for sweets, food and clothing. Also for petrol.

Bakers were exempt from the call-up. Wootton did not go short of bread (even though rationed), as there was plenty of flour to be had.

Young children could have fruit but as this was scarce, there was always a scramble for it.

Villagers who did not have big enough gardens, had allotments in the

"Dig for Victory" scheme. Each allotment was 10 poles (1 pole=30 1/4 square yards). These were to be found at Hall End, Bourne End at Frogshole (on brow of hill), Fields Road and Potters Cross (North Field opposite the Black Horse).

Anyone who did drive had a cover over the lights, the only light visible being through slits.

People went by phases of the moon. If it was a 'bombers' moon (a full moon) that is when trouble could be expected.

'Utility' was the only household ware that could be purchased. This was absolutely basic in style and unadorned.

Life, however, was not all dull. There were the dances at air force bases and army camps to which the local girls could be transported, including the American Air Force bases dotted around Bedford.

Wootton had its own concert party during the war. They played at functions being held in the village and venues outside. Daphne Addington played the piano and Joan Tysoe played the accordion.

Dances were held in the old school on the corner of Bedford Road and Church Road for Canadian and Scots airmen to meet each other and the villagers.

One evening two bombs fell opposite Kempston Barracks. A loudspeaker interrupted the film at the Granada cinema stating that customers could either stay or leave, as they wished. All the glass was smashed from the buildings in the High Street.

A burning aeroplane crash-landed in the field, owned by the Wiles family, at the rear of the bungalow (now converted into three), at the corner of Potters Cross and Bedford Road. Fortunately the pilot bailed out of the single seater but a lot of ammunition was left lying about in the field and the garden. This was hurriedly collected by officials. A crowd gathered to watch the burning wreckage. The crash made a large crater in which the children played.

After the war prefabs were built on this field and later the flats were built.

A contributor remembers a doodlebug flying over the bungalow but does not know where it landed. They all hid under the beds!

Then, of course, there were the gas masks that everyone carried around with them.

The Canadian army camp was based in Hall End Road. There were huts with searchlights and when the German bombers flew overhead, shouts of "put that light out" could be heard. When bombs where dropped on the old kiln pits on Tinkers' Corner shrapnel went through the barn near the houses opposite the Chequers and pieces were kept as souvenirs.

Travel was walking or cycling and it was common to walk to Bedford and back due to petrol rationing.

Special Constable Bill Green, who lived at Wood End, would knock on doors to tell people to turn the lights off.

All private house building stopped during the war although bricks were required for repairs and official building programmes, such as airfields. Brick making was initially a reserved occupation but Italian prisoners captured in North Africa were brought in to operate the brick kilns, thus making most of the original workers liable for call-up.

Incidentally, the London Brick vehicle fleet were also put to war work and were used for shipping munitions and supplies into local airfields.

V.E. Day was celebrated in the middle of Bedford Road and Cause End Road with amongst other goodies, ice cream. A bonfire was a great attraction.

Conclusion

We hope you have enjoyed this short journey into the history of our village. If you grew up here, we trust it brought back some memories and for those who have moved here, that it has been of interest. Since the Second World War, Wootton has expanded greatly and is set to expand some more during this new millennium. Let us hope the heart of the village remains and that this book has gone some way to preserving the stories and reminiscences from times past.

There will no doubt be gaps in our chronicle, events and persons we may not have mentioned. Maybe there is a follow-up book here somewhere. Who knows....

Appendices

1. 1309 Tax Return for Wootton

2. Muster List for 1539

3. Land Tax Returns for 1738

4. Major Landowners in 1800

5. 1838 the Main Landowners

6. 1832 Landowners' Acreage

7. 1881 Landowners/Farm Tenants

8. 1881 Populations of the Ends in Wootton

9. Population Table from 1801 to 1991

10. The Vicars of Wootton

11. The Church Bells

12. Wootton War Memorial

13. The Road Names of Wootton

Appendix 1 (Medieval Wootton chapter)

1309

Surname	No. of Taxpayers	Tax paid by people with that surname		
		s.	d.	
le Rous	1	16	8	Pilling Rousberry
Bottourte	1	13	7	Wootton Manor
Astei	6	12	5	
del Hoo	2	8	9	
le Sweyn	1	8	6	
de Sancto Edwardo	1	6	11	Studley Manor
West	1	6	10	
Aspelon	1	6	4	
de Hardwic	1	6	3	
Extraneo	1	6	3	
le Fyler	1	5	11	
Bernard	2	5	10	
Hammund	1	5	4	
Sutore	3	5	0	
le Loringe	2	4	11	
dei Hul	2	4	10	
atte Bourne	2	4	2	
Gobyoun	1	4	0	
Bydoun	1	3	10	
Roberd	2	3	10	
Godefrey	2	3	8	
de Craule	2	3	6	

Appendix 2

Muster List 1539

William Borne
Richard Stanbryg
John Brewton
Robert Pawll
Thomas Fokes
John Worsley
John Nytingall
Thomas Barber
John Fokes
Richard Maynard
John Lynwood
John Frankleyn

William Wheler
William Borrell
William Lyngerd
William Wallys
John Hart
Richard Maydenhed
Harry Tweg
William Cowper
Thomas Lan
William Stanbrig
Thomas Roowe
Richard Nityngale

John Stoot
William Hart
William Howcall
Hew Marram
John Worsley
Robert Wallys
Harry Saverall
Thomas Carter
William Stanbrig
Thomas Cowper
Thomas Borrage

The Muster Rolls for the Bedfordshire County Militia for 1539 listed 35 men in Wootton, which implies a population of about 200 people in 40 households.

Appendix 3

Land Tax Returns from 1738

Year Proprietors Assessed for Tax	1783 £	1797 £	1809 £	1820 £
Monoux, Payne & Buckworth	147	157	145	170
Berry	11	11	12	12
Joseph Robinson	32	31	24	24
Pemberton	15			
Dimmock		15	13	14
Sidney Sussex College	36	36	27	27
Lord Faulkland	44			
Motley Austin		44	41	
Samuel Cornish	19	19	20	20

Appendix 4

Landowners in Wootton

By 1800 the major ownership of the Wootton Manors was concentrated as follows:-

Manor	Owner
Wootton	Monoux
Bosums	Monoux
Canons	Monoux
Studleys	Monoux
Wootton Hoo	Lowndes
Keeley	Cornish
Pilling Rousberry	Sidney Sussex College
Pilling Shingay	Sidney Sussex College

Appendix 5

Landowners in Wootton

At the time of Enclosure in 1838, the two largest landowners were heirs to the Monoux estates: Colonel J. R. Buckworth (second husband of Mary Monoux) and Lucy Monoux (sister to Mary). Colonel Buckworth owned 899 acres, of this, 258 acres were granted to him in respect of his right to tithes as Lord of the Manor. Lucy Monoux held 531 acres, of this 210 acres were granted to her on enclosure in respect of her right to tithes.

Bosums Manor was purchased in 1514 by George Monoux, Wootton Manor acquired by the Monoux family in 1666. The Manors of Canons and Studleys were both purchased by Humphrey Monoux in 1658.

The land owned by Sidney Sussex College, mostly now part of Stewartby, was bestowed on the College in 1627 by Sir Francis Clark.

John Robinson was the grandson of Sir George Robinson, who had owned land in Wootton since 1783. In 1838, he owned 340 acres and farmed at Bourne End. The farm was offered for sale in 1857.

The Wootton Hoo estates were purchased in 1652 by the Lowndes family, who had considerable property in Berkshire. One branch of the family retained an interest in Wootton into the early twentieth century.

Keeley, the earlier Culy Manor, was owned from 1738 by Admiral Samuel Cornish.

Other landowners, at the time of the Enclosure were Charles Gambier 133 acres, J. B. Dimmock 122 acres and John Berry 112 acres.

Appendix 6

The Large Landowners in 1832

J. R. Buckworth	899 acres
Lucy Monoux	500 acres
Sidney Sussex College	359 acres
John Robinson	340 acres
J. B. Dimmock	122 acres
John Berry	112 acres

These six landowners owned about two-thirds of the land in 1832, at the time of Enclosure. Also the Vicar/Church owned 214 acres.

Landowners/Farm Tenants at the time of the 1881 Census

Name	Address	Acreage	No. of Employees
Barnard Dimmock	The Green	430	21
William Whitehouse	Pillinge	350	20
Ann Armstrong	Town Street Farm	315	11
Thomas Smith	Bourne End	306	10
Herbert Hunter	Bourne End	288	14
Samuel J. Swaffield	New Farm Cottage	210	12
William Joyce	Vicarage Farm	160	22

There are nine other farmers with less than 150 acres, listed in the 1881 census. Amongst these was John Burr at "the Hoos" with 58 acres. Five other employers are mentioned in the census, for example brickyards.

In addition to these farmers, their wives and children, there were 217 men and boys employed as agricultural labourers, four shepherds and four drivers of steam engines for threshing.

Appendix 8

Ends in Wootton

In the 1881 census there were 1302 people living in Wootton in 280 households. The households were dispersed in several ends.

	Households	People
Town Street	33	153
Hall End	28	132
Bot End	24	103
Bedford Road	23	102
Keeley	22	99
Cause End	21	110
Keeley Lane	19	100
Taggs End	17	80
The Green	14	69
Potty Cross	13	52
Wood End	12	46
Cranfield Road	12	45
Pillinge	9	44
Broadmead	9	43

Appendix 9

19th Century Census

The first census of 1801 recorded 732 people living in Wootton. Ten years later in 1811 there were 138 inhabited houses, 165 families and a population of 831 people in Wootton. The growth in population was very rapid: 13.7% more people lived in Wootton in 1811 than 10 years earlier. (Stewartby was of one third of the acreage of the original parish or of Wootton).

Year	Wootton (inc. Stewartby) Population	Wootton (inc. Stewartby) Dwellings
1801	732	
1811	831	138
1821	944	178
1831	1051	203
1841	1124	226
1851	1204	245
1861	1349	277
1871	1312	
1881	1302	279
1891	1253	268
1901	1252	255
1911	1394	
1921	1347	
1931	1551	379
1951	2968	636
1961	3061	925
1971	3918	1315
1991	4747	1925

Appendix 10

The Vicars of Wootton

1258	John of Dunstable	
1273	Nicholas	Died
1274	David of Wootton	Died
1301	Robert of Conington	Died
1328	John of Billesdon	Died
1348	William of Knyton	Resigned
1349	Richard of Knyton	Exchanged with next Vicar
1401	John Downe	Exchanged with next Vicar
1418	May: Matthew Barugh (sed. vac.)	
	August: John Barouse	
?	Matthew Skeerne	Died
1457	Thomas Barbour	Died
1490	John Lynne	Resigned
1497	Thomas Atkyn	Resigned
1499	Hugh Rere	
1534	Robert Hanslap	Deprived for marrying
1539	Reginald Werte	
1554	John Dave	
1562	Thomas Cox	
1581	Richard Levereck	Died
1600	Humphrey Tottenham	Died
1638	Alexander Hale	
1658	William Bunne	Died
1683	Thomas Cheyne	Resigned
1695	Dennis Cooling	Died
1711	Andrew Moore	Died
1719	February: German Pegg	
	August: John Slater	Died
1739	George Backhouse	Died

1775	John Welling	Died
1785	Thomas Gadsby	Resigned
1834	John Jenkyn	Resigned
1841	James Jenkyn	Resigned
1852	Frederick Neale	Died
1872	Thomas H. Vernon	Resigned
1880	Albert J. Foster	Resigned
1918	Charles E. Squire	Resigned
1940	Thomas Quigley	Resigned
1946	Charles W. F. Jebb	Resigned
1950	James F. Wilson	Resigned
1956	Ronald E. Thorp	Resigned
1964	Anthony J. Smith	Died
1975	John V. M. Kirkby	Resigned
1987	Christopher P. Strong	Resigned

The Parish of Wootton includes Stewartby, whose Ministers are technically Curates of Wootton too.

Appendix 11

The Church Bells

There are six bells at St. Mary's Church, they are hung in an oak frame dating from 1904 when the sixth bell was added.

The weight, note and inscription on each bell is as follows:-

The Treble bell weighs 746 lbs (340 kg) and is tuned in D. It is inscribed:- John Taylor & Co., Loughborough, Leicester 1904.

The second bell weighs 770 lbs (350 kg) and is tuned in C. It is inscribed:- William Emerton of Wootton Fecit 1779.

The third bell weighs 885 lbs (402 kg) and is tuned in B flat. It is inscribed J. Taylor & Co. Founders, Loughborough 1874.

The fourth bell weighs 1045 lbs (475 kg) and is tuned in A. It is inscribed:- Thomas Russell, William Russell Fecit. Stephen Hudson & Benjamin Rainbow Churchwardens 1736. Christopher Fleming, Thomas Fleming, John Slater.

The fifth bell weighs 1363 lbs (620 kg) and is tuned in G. It is inscribed:- J. Taylor & Co. Bellfounders, Loughborough 1874.

The Tenor bell weighs 1678 lbs (762 kg) and is tuned in F. It is inscribed:- God save our King 1641 IH.

The Origin of the Bells

The third and fifth bells were re-cast from bells previously cast in 1595 by John Dyer of Hitchin.

The sixth bell was cast by James Keene of Oxfordshire.

The second and fourth bells were cast in a foundry in Cause End Road, Wootton, where Astra House now stands.

Appendix 12

Wootton War Memorial

1939-45

S. Wright	J. Beard	F. Eastwood
G. Gooch	H. Pilsbury	R. Simms
G. E. Turland		

1914-18

O. G. Adams	T. Foulkes	E. W. Moore
H. F. Ashpole	F. J. Geanby	F. J. Moore
R. Ashpole	F. J. Gilbert	H. Moore
E. W. Ashpole	W. G. Goff	H. J. Pope
R. A. Allen	J. Goff	J. J. Parker
H. Bigg	G. A. Haynes	C. Parker
T. Billing	A. Harris	R. C. Pateman
T. W. R. Butler	G. W. Harris	W. Pilsbury
E. J. B. Church	J. W. Hutchings	S. Robinson
A. Denton	G. Keech	H. Robinson
T. Ellis	L. E. Lambert	E. Russell
E. Ellis	F. Loft	A. G. Steele
J. G. Evans	J. Lovell	S. J. Tysoe
L. T. L. Foster	F. Lovell	R. F. Church
F. J. Foulkes	J. Moore	

Appendix 13

Some of the Road Names of Wootton and their Origin

Named after the old Manors
Canons Close
Keeley Lane
Manor Road
Studley Road
Hoo Close

Local Landowners

Beauchamp Road	Family who owned land here in the 12th century
Cynthia Court	Wife of Sir Malcolm Stewart
Dimmock Road	Barnard Dimmock, farmer at Wootton Green
Farrell Road	Maurice Farrell, former Bishop of West Indies, lived at the Hoo
Lorraine Road	Albert of Lorraine, landowner at the time of the Domesday Book
Monoux Road	Lords of the manor from 1514, pronounced "Monux"
Payne Road	Successors to the Monoux family (Sir Coventry Payne and Sir Philip Payne)
Stewart Court	Sir Malcolm Stewart, founder of Stewartby

Local Vicars

Foster Way	Vicar from 1880 to 1918
Neale Way	Vicar from 1852 to 1872
Jenkyn Road	Vicars, John and James, from 1834 to 1852
Squires Road	Vicar from 1918 to 1940
Thorp Way	Vicar from 1956 to 1964

Parish Councillors

Barnes Road	Derek Barnes

Bellamy Road	Ron Bellamy
Halegate	Jack Hale
Popes Way	John Pope, Clerk to the Council
Sanders Way	Ern Sanders, also a County Councillor

Prominent Villagers of the Past

Browns Lane	Local Farmer, Keeley Corner
Emerton Way	Clock maker and bell founders
Mepham Road	J. P. and Schoolmaster
Russell Way	Clock makers and bell founders
Summerfield Drive	Caleb Summerfield, brick maker

Buildings

Old School Gardens
School Lane
St. Mary's Road
Tithe Barn Road

The Original Roads

Bedford Road	Hall End
Cause End Road	Potters Cross
Church Road/Row	
Fields Road	

$\mathcal{I}ndex$

Subject and Place Names

People